Before   *After*

Mark Connelly is that tried and true cliché: a lawyer who turned to writing as 'a much less demanding and less harmful way to spend one's time'. Mark is a Campaigns Director at GetUp! Australia (www.getup.org.au), an online community-based activist organisation of 400,000 members. He previously worked on John Kerry's presidential campaign in 2004.

His work has appeared in the *Manic Times* paper and website, *New Matilda* and the online policy magazine, *Insight*. In addition to his law degree from New York University School of Law, Mark holds a masters degree in Public Policy from University of Sydney.

Mark is American; however, growing up in New York allowed him to escape the general prohibition on irony put in place under the Reagan administration. He currently lives by the beach in Sydney with his very patient wife, Charmayne.

Happy Birthday
Richard
love
Mr + Mrs P.
x x.

THE LAST DECISION YOU'LL EVER MAKE

A groom's survival guide

MARK CONNELLY

Woof from Monty.

ALLEN&UNWIN

For my Char.
You were my first idea . . . the book came second.

First published in 2011

Allen & Unwin
83 Alexander Street
Crows Nest NSW 2065
Australia
Phone: (61 2) 8425 0100
Fax: (61 2) 9906 2218
Email: info@allenandunwin.com
Web: www.allenandunwin.com

Cataloguing-in-Publication details are available
from the National Library of Australia
www.trove.nla.gov.au

ISBN 978 1 74175 913 6

Internal design by Lisa White
Set in 11/15 pt Minion by Midland Typesetters, Australia

Printed in Great Britain by CPI Group (UK) Ltd, Croydon, CR0 4YY

10 9 8 7 6 5 4 3 2 1

The paper in this book is FSC certified.
FSC promotes environmentally responsible,
socially beneficial and economically viable
management of the world's forests.

CONTENTS

CONTENTS

THE PREFACE

HOW TO USE THIS BOOK

Start at the beginning, work your way through the middle, then finish up at the end. Or just jump around as you see fit.

NAMES

In general, names in this book have been changed to protect the innocent and guilty alike. However, the author was bored of the 'John and Jane' pseudonyms used by traditional wedding books so his brides and grooms are sometimes named after comic book and cartoon characters.

DISCLAIMERS

Irony Disclaimer

This book is prone to exaggeration, mischaracterisation, gross over- and understatement and similar forms of parody. This is done in the name of humour and irony, as well as to drive certain points home. The author respects the reader and believes that these satirical flourishes will be read in the spirit in which they were written. This warning is for any pretentious twits who will take something literally that was clearly not meant to be taken literally, and otherwise take offence at this book for not doling out *traditional* wedding advice, which it explicitly aims to ridicule. So please, spare the author self-righteous letters with lots of big words, as he has better things to do with his time.

Sexism Disclaimer

The key phrase here is 'in general and for the most part'. So, for any women reading this book who think the author has inappropriately attributed some universal characteristic to all women, or suggested some absolute mark of difference between men and women, please mentally insert the phrase 'in general and for the most part'. For example: women are [in general and for the most part] more interested in flowers, invitations and table settings than men. The author would insert these words himself in all such instances, but he is striving to maintain the economy of the chapters, along with the truly lyrical flow of his writing.

Women are neither the enemy nor the target of this book. The author likes women. In fact, he likes them so much he went and married one. If there is an enemy, it is a wedding industry that can drive both a bride and groom mad and cost them a fortune in the process. If there is a target, it is the absurdities that weddings create. The author will, to the best of his ability, help men understand more about the wedding process, the wedding industry and what their bride is going through. So please, read the book in that spirit before breaking out the torches and pitchforks.

Cultural Differences Disclaimer

The author frequently talks down spending a lot on a wedding or various parts of it, and even chides or mocks some who do. However, the author recognises that a lavish wedding is a cornerstone of family and community tradition in some cultures, such as with many Mediterranean families (e.g., Greek and Italian weddings). The author has no issues with these traditions and has no wish to defy or ridicule them. Often in such cases, the bride's parents have been saving for the wedding since their daughter was born, so this doesn't raise the same financial issues for the couple. A major premise of this book is that couples are getting married later in life and are increasingly taking on the financial and planning burdens of their own wedding. While this book is meant for all couples, certain sections have particular relevance for those who do not have major financial backing from culturally prideful parents.

Third Person Disclaimer

Yes, the author refers to himself as 'the author' above and that's terribly pretentious. It also suggests that there is someone else out there actually typing this stuff up, because 'the author' has lots of money and better things to do with his time. He has neither. 'I' just seemed a little too personal, whereas 'the author' maintains some kind of professional distance. Perhaps it can create some legal distance as well. I don't really know, and neither does the author.

THE INTRODUCTION

Abandon All Hope,
Ye Who Enter Here

To paraphrase Matt Damon in *Dogma*,
wedding planning is 'the most exhausting activity
one can engage in, outside of soccer'.

. . . 'Nough said.

SETTING EXPECTATIONS

In Dante's *Divine Comedy*, 'Abandon all hope, ye who enter here' is inscribed on the gates of hell. Don't worry, the wedding process isn't *that* horrible. I just thought I'd set your expectations low, so that everything to come won't seem so bad.

In many ways, proposing to your loving partner *is* the last decision you'll ever make. Not that all decisions will now be made *for* you (though some will), but they won't be solely yours any more. You've already experienced this with small decisions, like whether to see a movie that stars Clint Eastwood or Meryl Streep (damn, forgot about *The Bridges of Madison County*—why, Clint, why?). It will now happen more with big decisions, like what car to buy and where you're going to live. The wedding process puts this unsettling change into stark relief, because there are so many decisions and you tend to have very little say in any of them.

Despite the mythology, back in the day (50 years ago) weddings used to be fairly simple affairs. They were often held in the backyard of the bride's parents, with finger sandwiches, punch and maybe some grog. Who knows how the one-upmanship (or one-upbrideship) began, but it's fostered ever-escalating expectations. While some wedding professionals claim to lament this, the message is drowned out by every other aspect of their advice (all the things you *must have* for your wedding). So, you need to teach your bride one of the most useful phrases in life: *screw 'em*. That's right, screw the wedding professionals, screw your family, screw your friends, screw Brad and Angelina, screw 'em all. It's your wedding and what anyone else did or wants you to do doesn't matter. Allow me to demonstrate:

Bride: But Belinda and her husband had a butterfly release at their wedding and—
You: Yeah, screw 'em.
Bride: Screw who?
You: Belinda and what's his name.
Bride: What do you mean, 'screw 'em'?
You: I mean, screw 'em. Because I'm not getting married to Belinda, What's-his-name, or anyone else on the sixth of March. So, what do *you* want? Not what your friends had or think you should have. Not what your mother had or wishes she had when she got married. What do *you* really want? To figure that out, first you have to learn to say 'screw 'em'.

Feel better? It would be nice if you could say all that, but I presume you want this marriage to actually happen, so best to make the point more delicately with your bride. But you and I can still say 'screw 'em'.

SCREW 'EM DISCLAIMER
Your ability to use 'screw 'em' may be limited by several factors, such as whether your in-laws are paying for the wedding. Such is the burden of financial assistance (unless you're a major bank getting bailed out by the government). Certainly, anyone without a financial stake in the wedding can be screwed with impunity. Also, note that 'screw 'em' is something for you and your partner in the privacy of your own wedding planning—not, for example, to your mother-in-law's face.

UNDER PRESSURE

'[B]ut remember, this should be an enjoyable time!' (Love 2007, p. 9) Too many books talk about what an 'enjoyable', 'special' and 'fun' time the wedding process is. This can put the pressure on, making you feel like you're doing something wrong if you don't feel all the unmitigated joy of painstakingly filling out name cards. On the contrary, if you and your bride are feeling wedding stress, you're not alone. Psychologists have a list of stressful life events to help gauge when people are most likely, in clinical terms, to 'go nutty'. It tells us that few of life's troubles and strife are more stressful than getting married.

STRESSFUL LIFE EVENTS (100 = MOST STRESSFUL)	
100	Death of spouse
73	Divorce
65	Marital separation
63	Jail term
63	Death of close family (except spouse)
53	Major personal injury or illness
50	**Marriage**
47	Being fired
39	Sexual difficulties
38	Change in finances
37	Death of close friend
30	Foreclosure of mortgage

Three of the events more stressful than getting married have to do with losing your wife (to divorce, separation or death). Perhaps it would be better to have never loved at all than to have loved and lost, as love seems to kick you coming and going. Also, note that two things that *didn't* make the most-stressful list are 'loneliness' and 'carefree sex'.

Scanning down the list, we see that getting married is *more* stressful than a change in finances, sexual difficulties and the death of a close friend, which just shows what kind of friend you are. That means your partner may find it easier to deal with her bridesmaid's demise than her refusal to wear the right shoes (not that I'm making suggestions). Weddings are also more stressful than a mortgage foreclosure or getting fired. So, all those people who lost their homes and jobs in the global financial crisis should be damn glad they didn't find love too, or they'd be popping Xanax like Tic Tacs.

THE WEDDING INDUSTRY

In his farewell address, President Dwight D Eisenhower warned people of the military-industrial complex. This book warns about the 'matrimonial-industrial complex'. To paraphrase General Eisy, *we must guard against the acquisition of unwarranted influence, whether sought or unsought, by the matrimonial-industrial complex. The potential for the disastrous rise of misplaced power exists and will persist.* This complex is formed when eager young couples and their families meet head-on with wedding magazines, websites and books, the mavens of wedding etiquette and a cabal of businesses eager to exploit the couple's desire for a 'special day' into an aneurism-producing, cash-sucking vacuum.

For example, one wedding professional scoffs at the 'punch-and-cake' receptions that your mother may have had (Weatherly 2005, p. xii). Now, what was wrong with punch and cake? Do you know anybody who doesn't like punch and cake? For decades the matrimonial-industrial complex has fuelled a wedding arms race among family, friends and neighbours to extravagantly lift the cost of weddings. Don't buy into it (except for buying this book for your family, friends and neighbours). At the end of the day, getting married surrounded by the people you care about is much more important than the quality of the champagne, the gilding on the wedding program or showing up your friends.

THE PERFECTION PERCEPTION

I don't believe in 'the perfect wedding'. It's like 'satisfaction guaranteed', 'all natural' and 'GST: never, ever'. It's an absolute promise, in which you have no faith yet still passively accept. It's a glossy, sterile, empty, greeting-card, Stratford Wife concept devoid of warmth, personality or imagination. It suggests some universal ideal of wedding that everyone should strive for, when everything that will make *your* wedding memorable are those things particular to you, your family and friends. Still, like the models in fashion magazines, airbrushed to a fraction of their true selves, bridal magazines airbrush the picture of the perfect wedding into your bride's brain. If you can get her to realise and *accept* that not every one of the thousand details of your wedding will be cover-shot perfect, she might relax a little. *Don't let the perfect be the enemy of the wonderful.*

'Why So Serious?'

One wedding book dubs it-self 'a guerrilla wedding planning guide' (a book with the becalming title *Stop! Don't Plan a Wedding Without this Book*, Weatherly 2005, p. xi) and describes the wedding process as 'a planning feat of such precision and detail that it would make military generals weep' (p. xii). If you treat wedding planning like a war it will feel like a war, especially with an 'us vs them' mentality. That's a painful stance to take with wedding professionals (despite what I say about them) and a very unhealthy one to take with family and friends. Against the fairytale wedding script laid out in the books and magazines, some things will undoubtedly go wrong on your wedding day. The only thing that *ruins* things is believing that any of the bullshit actually matters. If you and your bride refuse to take things too seriously, then you've donned an impenetrable suit of armour impervious to all wedding stuff-ups.

> **A NOD TO HEATH**
>
> 'Why so serious?' is a little nod to Heath Ledger as the Joker in *The Dark Knight*, which leads to a broader point. One of the greatest sins in Australia is to take yourself too seriously. This is a great advantage when entering into wedding planning. Hold fast to it.

A Little Perspective

You may now be experiencing the proposal hangover. The joy of celebrating your future lives together in mutual love and understanding has suddenly turned into a wedding. Before diving in, it's important to get some *perspective*—the thing you lose right before mutual love and understanding.

Consider the following advice to brides, from *Stop! Don't Plan a Wedding Without this Book*: 'Now, if your calligrapher is waiting on your envelopes and they've been lost in the mail for a week already, you have my permission to have a minor meltdown' (Weatherly 2005, p. 17).

Ironically, this passage strives to give brides perspective on what they should and should not freak out about. To my thinking, if you're getting calligraphic wedding invitations you've already lost the plot. So, I offer the following distinctions for you and your partner, to provide some *real* perspective:

FREAK-OUT WORTHY	NOT FREAK-OUT WORTHY
Your reception venue burns down a week before the wedding.	The florist uses pink instead of white baby's breath in the flower arrangements.

TRAGIC	NOT TRAGIC
A member of your wedding party has to go to hospital.	The impact on your wedding of a member of your wedding party going to hospital.

URGENT	NOT URGENT
Moving up the wedding, so the bride's dying father can walk his girl down the aisle before he passes (a real story).	Your wedding invitations are late to the calligrapher.

If your bride is having a 'minor meltdown' over something that seems trivial in the scheme of things, conjure up a true calamity for comparison to help give her some perspective. If a real calamity strikes, do what men do best and ignore the problem in the hope it will sort itself out.

STEAMROLLER BABY

The traditional wedding books talk about the importance of 'open and honest communication' and the need for 'discussion', 'compromise' and 'understanding'. This 'communication' is when your bride tells you what the wedding will be like, followed by a 'discussion' of your views, where you will learn to 'compromise' and 'understand' how it's going to be. Fair enough. As men, we haven't given much thought to our wedding. Some women have been thinking about it since they were little girls, shaping wads of tissue paper into makeshift veils. We have to accept that this day, and everything about it, just means a whole lot more to them than it does to us. It also involves a lot of things—like flowers, clothing, embroidery, table settings, and so on—that are more their territory.

That doesn't mean we don't care at all, or that there aren't specific things we care a lot about (like not playing UB40's 'Red Red Wine' for the first dance). We should have *some* input, even if it's largely a veto role. It does mean that it's best to pick your battles. Don't get caught in arguments about things you don't really care about, when you know she does. On things you do care about, lead with the fact that there are very few things you *do* care about and it's only fair that you get your way on some of them.

What happens if you're getting steamrolled on *everything* by your bride or her family? Maybe you're into the wedding planning (not that there's anything wrong with that). Maybe there are some things you definitely do *not* want (you're not sure what a 'colour scheme' is, but 'crimson' has you worried). When you're a lawyer, like me, friends come to you all the time with their grievances. I always ask them, 'Assuming you have a case, is it worth it?' Litigation is expensive, time-consuming and often nasty, plus there's no guarantee of success and that success is rarely satisfying. Battles with your bride and her family are similar—generally, I say it's not worth the grief and bad feelings.

> **GROOM AFFIRMATION**
> If it helps, stare into the mirror and repeat the phrase 'I am not a prop' over and over to yourself.

Still, you have some skin in the game too, and while your opinions shouldn't rule they should matter. You're more than just a prop. If you're repeatedly getting steamrolled then you may have to brandish your nukes: remind everyone that they need you to show up to have a wedding. Just remember, while nuclear weapons are a great deterrent, they're never meant to be used. If the eighties Matthew Broderick classic *War Games* taught us anything, it's that no one wins at nuclear war (as noted by Joshua, the AI computer: 'A strange game. The only winning move is not to play').

THE ETIQUETTE TOURNIQUET

As men, we rightly scoff at 'etiquette'. First, it's hard to spell. Second, it stirs in us a kind of primal rebellion. Thousands of years ago we were dragged from our caves, shaved of excessive body hair, clothed in polyester and began talking in full sentences (except at major sporting events). Etiquette feels like the last battleground for hairy, shirtless, monosyllabic maleness. Still, etiquette is the watchword of most wedding books, so I would like to step back and distinguish two very different meanings.

Jane Austen Etiquette

This is a bunch of stodgy, tight-arse rules that last had relevance in the novels of Jane Austen. You never get a justification beyond 'that's just how things are done'. In many cases, it's just how your parents did it and maybe your grandparents. It's also funny how adhering to this type of etiquette always seems to cost you more. Wedding books quote 'manners', 'etiquette' and 'tradition' without ever questioning what purpose they still serve. I want to know who makes these rules. I demand to know their purpose. And if they can 'say so', we can say different. At various places in this book I declare some etiquette rules null and void. If you agree and take a stand, then we can begin to turn the tide on *Sense and Sensibility*.

> **SEEING SENSE**
>
> Author Seth Grahame-Smith took an axe to a Jane Austen classic (quite literally) in his novel *Pride and Prejudice and Zombies*. In addition to her 'comedy of manners' with the irascible Mr Darcy, Elizabeth Bennett must contend with the 'hordes of flesh-eating undead' afflicting her small English town. It's since been followed by *Sense and Sensibility and Sea Monsters*, by Ben H. Winters. I only have one thing to say: why didn't I think of this?

Considerate Etiquette

This simply means being considerate of other people. Scoff at it if you like, but do so at your own peril. Many a family feud was instigated by inadvertent slights doled out by etiquette-scoffing couples at their own wedding. But, if you make an effort to consider others in your planning, no one should fault you for flouting convention (and if they do, that's their hang-up). For example, if you decide to have your wedding at the top of Mount Vesuvius, make arrangements for any older or disabled guests (helicopter?). Don't let etiquette get in the way of what you want for your wedding, but also put yourself in your guests' shoes when planning so everyone enjoys themselves. In the end, that's what makes a wedding tops and that's *good etiquette.*

STARTING POINTS

You don't need to reinvent the wheel on all things wedding to have a personal experience, and trying to do so will greatly add to you burden.

Traditions

While you shouldn't feel stifled by wedding traditions, they're not a bad place to start. Remember, there won't be many things that you actually care about in the wedding. In most cases, you just want the planning and chores to go as quickly and smoothly as possible. For instance, when my partner and I prepared our invitations, we took the format straight out of a traditional wedding book and just tweaked it for our circumstances. Why? Because neither of us really cared how the invite was worded and that was the easiest way to get it done. So, for things you don't care about too much you might as well go the traditional route, or at least use the traditional route as your starting point and go from there.

Other People's Weddings

One way for you and your bride to start discussing the type of wedding you want is to talk about weddings you've been to and what you've liked and not liked about them (together with your partner you can abuse the choices of friends and loved ones). That doesn't mean copying someone else's wedding—of course, every wedding is a truly unique, beautiful experience, as individual as a snowflake, or DNA at a crime scene. It's a matter of pulling out particular features of different weddings that you either admired (beach location, ice sculptures, buffet service) or detested (cheesy DJ, church wedding, sit-down dinner). It won't get you all the way there but it's a good place to start, especially if you're stuck.

1

THE PROPOSAL

The Last Decision You'll Ever Make

'*Remember, just as foreplay opens the way for sex, your engagement foreshadows your marriage*'
(Shervan and Sniechowski 2005, p. 25).

. . . Remember, just as the engagement is so crucial for women, it can often be tedious and frustrating for men.

TRUE ROMANCE

Romantic gestures have two positive effects. Sure it's nice for your partner to get flowers, jewellery or dinner cooked for her. What's even better for her is telling her friends about the nice thing you did, so she can make them jealous. This may sound petty, but it's no different than the competition men have over many, many things.

You want your proposal to be memorable and romantic, in the true definition of romance: making her girlfriends jealous because she has such a great guy. This can lead to an unsustainable spiral of one-upmanship (proposal hyperinflation) that makes it increasingly hard for your proposal to measure up. However, the key is not grandness, expense, zaniness or media coverage. The key is *meaning*—that the proposal be meaningful to you and her in some way particular to the two of you.

ARE YOU READY (FOR MRS RIGHT)?

How do you know when you've found the right person? Some wedding magazines feature readiness tests, asking questions about eye colour, secondary schools, pet names and home towns. It's more like information required for committing identity theft than anything useful for knowing whether you're ready to make a lifetime commitment to someone.

Are You Ready?

When it comes to readiness it's easier to point out the bad signs, like the ultimatum: you get married, or she's leaving. If you're getting married with a gun pointed to your head, then you should really think very carefully about what

THE ULTIMATUM

Consider this sad tale from *Sleepless in Seattle* (Annie is Meg Ryan and Dennis is the guy who played Frasier's brother on *Frasier*):

> Annie: I mean, why did you get married? Was it all trumpets and fireworks and . . .
>
> Dennis: I got married because Betsy said we had to break up or get married. So we got married.

you're doing. You have two people's lives in your hands, possibly more.

Another bad sign is pre-marital affairs. There is a theory that the engagement provides a window for having casual sex with other women to 'get it out of your system'. This is dubious logic, as cheating tends to be habit forming. If you come up with good excuses while you're engaged (sowing your wild oats), you will be quite capable of coming up with excuses once you're married ('*she* was coming on to *me*'). I enjoyed many years as a bachelor. A sign of readiness for me was that I no longer had any desire to crowd up to a sweaty bar and wait twenty minutes to pay eight bucks for a domestic beer in the hopes of impressing some vapid solarium junkie into coming home with me. If you just can't give up the single life, then maybe you shouldn't.

Is She the One?

There's no magic answer to whether you've found the right person. For men, I reckon it's

HONEY TRAPS

Don't forget, if you cheat, you could get caught, and not just by your own ineptitude or traditional detective services. One 'honey traps' service will stick a 'honey' on you to see if you take the bait: 'An attractive agent will approach your partner to flirt, eventually asking for a phone number and second date. We will then give you a comprehensive report.'

when we've found someone who saves us from ourselves. (This advice is both seemingly profound and vague enough to shield me from any legal claims. I'm afraid your divorce and any financial losses you suffer therein are entirely on your head.) I also like the way Vikram Chandra put it in his novel *Sacred Games*: 'We are all fools . . . To find one person who forgives you for this, that is big. That is great' (2007, p. 624).

THE PROPOSAL PARADOX

Expectations are a bitch. If you're at that stage in your relationship when your proposal might come at any time, it may be *expected* at any time (or all the time). If you take your girlfriend to a really nice restaurant, on a trip to Europe, or bring her breakfast in bed, your kind efforts may be overshadowed by your failure to propose. Of course, she can't acknowledge that to you, so you'll have no earthly idea why she's so pouty. And it's not like you can preface every special occasion with: 'By the way, I just wanted you to know that I will *not* be proposing to you now.' That's what we call a *mood killer*.

This brings us to the *proposal paradox*: most women want the man to propose, of his own accord, but want it done to her timetable and on her terms. Unfortunately, the man is usually in the dark as to his girlfriend's timetable. We're just supposed to *know*, through some psychic power or cosmic signal. Complicating matters is that pressuring a man into something is a sure-fire way of getting him *not* to do it. This unwelcome prodding can come from outside as well as in: 'So, when are you two moving in together?' 'When are you getting hitched?' 'When are you having kids?' Anytime a man hears these questions, he mentally backs up such plans by six to twelve months.

Are there ways out of this paradox? Hint dropping is very important. Is she pointing out rings she likes? Is she flipping through wedding magazines? Is she talking incessantly about people getting engaged or married? Eventually, the hints become less roundabout: 'You know, it's really just a matter of you asking me. You *know* that, don't you?' Fortunately, even when hints lose their subtlety, the sense that the proposal was inspired by your love, and your love alone, is preserved. A little self-delusion is a good way out of a paradox.

PROPOSAL CLASSIFICATION

To provide some guidance, I have developed a general proposal classification system.

Traditional: Expensive Restaurant

We've seen it in a thousand movies and TV shows: the fancy decor, the mood lighting, the chilled champagne. There is nothing wrong with the traditional approach, especially if you're with a traditional kind of girl (i.e., she *didn't* experiment at uni), and particularly if the restaurant or the day has special meaning for you. The surprise factor here may be low, unless you frequently dine at the finest restaurants in town and order pricey French champagne, but not all women like surprises.

> **DINING OUT**
>
> It's strange that two main reasons people are taken to nice restaurants are proposals and dismissals.

Travel: Paris

If you're at the proposal stage in your relationship your partner might have some inkling that you *could* propose on your trip, but you can choose the time and place and do particular things to make it memorable. Paris is a great city for proposals. Sure it's a cliché, but Paris, like New York, is one of those remarkable places that transcends cliché. The best course is to choose some place special to your girlfriend (maybe she studied art in Rome and her painting of the Trevi Fountain hangs on the wall—so there's a good spot). Just pray you don't get a random security check at the airport exposing that unmistakable black velvet box to your girlfriend.

Adventure: Skydiving

Are you and your partner thrillseekers? A submariner of my acquaintance set up an underwater treasure chest for a scuba-diving session with his partner, and when she opened it a sign asking her to marry him floated out. Another friend of mine proposed to his partner after they jumped out of a plane. If he could face death, he could face marriage. Surprise is built into these proposals, along with adrenaline. It's a good way to go for that Mountain Dew–chugging, X Games girl in your life.

Theatrical: Bird Show

I was minding my own business at the Taronga Zoo bird show one day when the trainer selected a young woman as a volunteer. She held out a coin, and a bird swooped down and plucked it from her hand. When the bird went back to return the coin, it deposited a diamond ring in its stead. Her boyfriend kneeled and proposed, the girl said 'Yes', and we all applauded. A unique approach, with a certain theatrical flair. As with all public proposals, though, you better be sure of your answer. Nothing like getting shat on at the bird show.

Stupid: Sporting Event

Please do not do the sports stadium proposal. This might have been a clever way to ask a girl to marry you before it was done about a million times. Also, when you've just wolfed down a meat pie and stale beer is keeping your shoes stuck to the concrete flooring, you know it's not the height of romance.

Homey: Breakfast in Bed

You and your girl may be private people. You may love nothing more than lounging in bed, curled up together watching movies or bad television. This lends itself to the breakfast-in-bed proposal. One word of caution: even the loungy girl might want something grander for her proposal. One man about to pop the question in bed was shattered when his girlfriend chose that moment to blurt out how lame it is when guys propose over breakfast in bed. So, you might want to check with her sister or a close friend before proceeding with this approach.

Special Spot

A special spot proposal means that you take your girlfriend to a place that has particular meaning to her, you or both of you, or has some spectacular feature (top of a mountain, seaside lookout, the resting place of Spike Milligan, etc.). A great example of this is discussed below.

A GREAT PROPOSAL

In the very early days of their relationship, Destro overheard Baroness say that the man she marries should know her well enough to propose to her at her favourite place in the world. At a completely separate time, Destro overheard Baroness talking about this little cliffside pub in Ireland, on the Ring of Kerry, with fantastic views of the sea. She reckoned it was her favourite place in the world. It took a great deal of research for Destro to find out what the 'Ring of Kerry' was (it's a road that runs through numerous towns), let alone the particular pub she was talking about. Then he employed subterfuge. Baroness thought they were going to a tropical destination. At the airport, Destro announced a change of plans. They were flying to Ireland (he made alternative clothing arrangements).

After arriving, he drove with her along the Ring of Kerry, asking her continuously whether *this* was her favourite spot on earth (knowing all along where it was). 'No,' she would say, quizzically (both of her remarks were so long ago, so far apart and so off the cuff that she honestly did not know what he was up to).

Finally they arrived at the little pub with the spectacular view. He asked her again whether *this* was her favourite spot. 'Yes,' she said. And then he asked her to marry him. She said, 'Yes,' again.

What was so great about this proposal? First, he listened. Yes, a man actually *listened* to his girlfriend, and listened attentively, on multiple occasions, and remembered what she said years later. The rarity of this alone would have been a proposal triumph. Second, the first of her comments came very early in the relationship, which meant that, even then, he thought this could be the woman he would marry, and that's romantic. Third, he chose a spot that had particular meaning for her. Fourth, there was a tremendous amount of thought and work that went into this. Finally, he managed to maintain an element of surprise, even though he proposed to her in exactly the way she had said she wanted—that's a neat trick.

After the lengths Destro went to for the proposal, he explained to Baroness that his job was done and he did not intend to be involved in the wedding planning. The Baroness actually accepted this, which just goes to show how far a great proposal can get you.

NERVES: AIM BETWEEN THE GRANTS

Some of the traditional proposal advice is truly classic: 'try to remain as calm and normal as possible' (Love 2007, p. 8). It's like the safety presentation on airplanes. That's all well and good, dill weed, but when the cabin pressure drops and I'm hurtling at 300 metres per second towards a large brown landmass, putting my head between my knees and keeping calm aren't going to help much.

The Answer

You really shouldn't be nervous about the answer, unless: 1) you're asking because she's pregnant, or 2) you're a character on a TV show trying to build dramatic tension. The fact is, by the time you ask the question she's probably dropped some subtle (and not-so-subtle) hints about her answer, as noted above. The nerves are more about the moment itself. Did you choose the right place, the right time? Are you doing it the right way? This moment will be etched in time, for her especially, and you're scared that you're going to screw it up.

The Moment

To take some terror out of the moment, think about what you're going to say ahead of time. It doesn't have to be a speech. The good old '————, I love you, will you marry me?' works pretty good. It's not *how* you ask the question—it's the fact that you're asking it. Rehearsing is fine, but practising a lot will make it sound, well, *practised*. Remember how charmingly befuddled Hugh Grant is in all those movies your partner dragged you to. (Don't you just want to shoot him between the eyes?)

Secretly, I think women want to see a bit of nerves. If you just walk up with a Cary Grant swagger and a cocky smile and say, 'Marry me, darling,' she'll think you don't have much riding on this. When you agreed to move in with her, you probably said something like, 'Well, we're spending five nights a week together anyway, it will be a lot easier and we'll save on rent.' Men are practical creatures and that's just how we think. But for many women, 'moving in' represents an important step in the relationship, and you just turned it into a budgeting measure. A similarly casual tone or rational calculus in your proposal will not be easily forgiven or forgotten. So, when you propose, aim between the Grants (Cary and Hugh).

HONOUR *HER* MOTHER AND FATHER

I am a proponent of asking for her father's blessing, under most circumstances. What do you have to lose? Generally, your engagement is not going to come as a huge surprise. If you call her father to arrange a meet-up without your partner, he's going to know what it's about and will probably take it easy on you—unless he feels like screwing with you a little (it's his last chance, in a way).

Of course, these days it isn't really so much about permission as respect. It's a recognition that there were a lot of awkward, painful years between birth and his daughter becoming the woman you fell in love with, and this is the man who had to put up with all of her crazy teenage crap.

> **AWKWARD YEARS**
>
> There's a memorable quote from a very forgettable Paul Reiser movie called *Bye Bye, Love*:
>
> Donny: It's a very awkward age for girls.
> Dave: Really? What age is that?
> Donny: Thirteen to 35, very awkward.

Fearing the Answer

What if her father isn't your biggest fan or you have reasons to believe he won't give his blessing? It's still probably best to ask. Even if he says no he's got to give you some credit for coming to him, especially if you have reason to fear his response. You might not get her father to like you or agree with your marriage, but at least he can respect you and that's not a bad place to start. You'll also get credit with your girlfriend by showing that you recognise the importance of her family to her and by doing something quite painful for her sake. If your future father-in-law wants to tee up a you-versus-him showdown for his daughter's affection, you've just started things off on the high ground and put him on the back foot.

GUY TALK

Men don't discuss things much, but there are a few recognised protocols. For instance, back in uni my friend Clark wanted to start seeing Lois, who had dated Lex for a while (yes, it's very *Home and Away*). Clark and Lex weren't close, but travelled in the same circles. So, Clark went to talk to Lex about it, not to ask for permission but just to clear the air. This avoided potential awkwardness down the track and, more importantly, it reinforced Clark's image as a 'stand up guy' to Lex and others. This became known as one of the '*Maxim* rules' (after the men's magazine): if you want to date or hook up with your friend's ex, you have to ask him first. The corollary of the rule is, he has to say yes.

For women who object to the apparent territoriality of this, please note that the ex-boyfriend does not have a *claim* to his ex-girlfriend, which is why he has to say 'Yes' even if it bothers him. It's about being upfront. One might say it's done out of consideration for the ex-boyfriend's feelings, but us guys don't admit to stuff like that.

The Talk

Be warned that according to (stupid) etiquette again, your partner's parents have the right to talk to you about finances. This seems a bit old-fashioned, especially as your partner should be aware of your finances and is fully capable of weighing them in her own decision. (I may be a bit defensive, as shortly before I proposed to my girlfriend I was made redundant from my job as a corporate lawyer and decided to embark on a writing career, with no discernible prospects.) In short, I don't think her parents are entitled to bank account details or your last tax return, but a general discussion about how you *and your partner* plan to make your way in the world is not unreasonable.

Womyn

You probably shouldn't talk to her father before proposing if your girlfriend would be greatly offended (i.e., it represents a paternalistic societal paradigm that has held women back for centuries). In that case, you and your partner can go to *both* of her parents afterwards, to ask for their blessing *together*.

WHAT IF SHE SAYS 'NO'?

That's a tough one. First off, if she said 'No' then I really don't see you buying this book, but no refunds either way.

'No' doesn't necessarily mean 'No' forever. Women are complicated and she may have said 'No' for reasons that have nothing to do with how she feels about you or what she actually wants. Talk to her, try to find out what her reservations are and try not to do this in a desperate, pleading or drunken manner. If it's a 'No, because . . .' answer, then do what you can to remedy the issue (her parents' disapproval, your unemployment or those skinny sideburns that follow your jawline around to your chin).

If it's a 'No' because she doesn't love you and it's time to break up, then that just sucks. I hardly need to tell you what to do. But, when you go out and get absolutely rat-arsed for the next month and try to score with as many women as possible, you need to bring at least one friend along who'll make sure you don't do any permanent damage to your body, mind or credit rating—and *absolutely no drunk-dialling your ex*.

Hey, but who could say 'No' to you, Big Boy? Especially when you slip her that ring.

PROPER ANNOUNCEMENT

I was vaguely aware of wedding announcements, but a newspaper announcement for an engagement? My general reaction to public notices for personal stuff is, who really cares? It's either for people I know, in which case I'd rather tell them myself than have them find out while scanning the classifieds for a new muffler; or it's for people I don't know, and in that case I'm a little creeped out that they're reading about my personal life. If your bride or the parents insist, I've my own sample announcement based on the traditional format:

Mr and Mrs Lachlan Oliver Twittletwat, Vaucluse, New South Wales announce the engagement of their daughter Miss Herminia Nostalgia Twittletwat to Mr Pookie 'Meth' Bigbooty, son of Mr and Mrs Jango Bigbooty of Cabramatta, New South Wales. A November wedding is planned.

Miss Twittletwat is a graduate of the Paris Finishing School for Uninformed Virgins and is a floral arranger for Fatuous Florists in Double Bay, New South Wales. Mr Bigbooty is a graduate of Cabramatta Basement Primary and is a local distributor of chemically enhanced pharmaceuticals.

2

THE RING

The 'Fifth C'

'The diamond, in its brilliance and purity, is representative of the core maiden self, the most innocent aspect that lives inside a woman. It is Psyche, the pure virginal dewdrop, the maiden before she is transformed into a queen'
(Paul 2000, p. 35).

... Funny how much 'innocence' and 'purity' run you these days, especially compared to the cost of vice and impurity in Kings Cross.

BLING IS BLUNG

For those tragically addicted to the mainstreaming of previously hip language, I will not at any time use the word 'bling', or the phrase 'bling bling', except to inform you now that I will not be using them. First, it's a silly word to begin with. Second, it long ceased to be cool in the very hip-hop, urban culture from which it arose. Finally, it was killed by the very people who expect to see it in a chapter on rings in a wedding book and by those wedding writers who oblige them. Peace out.

The 'Fifth C' originates from an argument I had with my partner about the traditional 'Four Cs' of diamonds. I insisted one of them was 'Cost'. A foolish presumption on my part, as the diamond industry is hardly going to promote cost as a relevant factor. For the record, the Four Cs of diamonds are: Carat, Cut, Clarity and Colour.

But, as men, we are forced to confront the unspoken 'Fifth C'—COST. Diamonds may be a girl's best friend, but they are a financial kick in the balls for would-be grooms.

You may be tempted to spend like a government trying to win re-election, partly because you don't yet realise how much the wedding will cost (read ahead). Diamonds may be forever; just make sure your debt isn't.

THE FOUR Cs

Here's a basic rundown on the traditional Four Cs of diamond quality.

Carat

Not like we didn't know it, but size does matter, and in this instance you *can* pay for enlargement but it's a bit more.

It's a pretty simple principle: the more carats, the larger it is, the more expensive it is (all else being equal). One carat is equal to one fifth of a gram. You might also hear of 'points', where one carat equals 100 points. Carat is the easiest of the Cs to grasp, so it's useful to check out different diamonds in the same carat weight to help you appreciate the other factors that go into the cost and quality of a stone.

Cut

The way a diamond is cut determines its brilliance (how it captures and reflects light) and gives it that diamond sparkle. It's cut into a series of neighbouring angled surfaces, perhaps 57 or 58. Cut is considered by some to be the most important of the four Cs, but let's face it: to real people it's probably carat.

Clarity

You'd think *clear* was presumed when it comes to diamonds, but apparently there are degrees of clearness. This refers to the tiny imperfections (or 'inclusions') that occur naturally inside the stone. The clarity scale runs from 'Included' (I)—flaws visible to the naked eye—to 'Slightly Included' (SI), 'Very Slightly Included' (VSI) and 'Very, Very Slightly Included' (VVSI) (sounds like *Bill & Ted's*

SHAPE UP

The 'shape' of a diamond is different from, but related to, the 'cut' and is not technically one of the Four Cs (for at least one obvious reason). Diamond shapes include: round brilliant, marquis, heart shaped, emerald, pear shaped, square and oval. Round brilliant is the traditional and most popular shape for a diamond (at least 75 per cent of cut diamonds), especially for an engagement ring.

Non-Non-Non-Heinous Diamond Clarity Ratings). Beyond that are 'Internally Flawless' (IF) and 'Flawless' (F) diamonds, which are 'very, very likely' out of your price range.

Generally speaking, you won't want an 'included' diamond for an engagement ring, so that leaves diamonds in the SI to VVSI range. This is where reason should grab you by the scruff of the neck. Unless all your partner's friends walk around with those funny jeweller eyepieces, I wouldn't throw down an extra month's salary just to avoid a few, practically invisible imperfections. If you're on a budget, or trading off against the other Cs, an SI or VSI diamond will be cheaper than a VVSI diamond and will still have no visible flaws. You probably care more about how it looks than what's written on some certificate.

Colour

You'd think the colour would just be *clear*, and that we've covered that already under 'Clarity', but they like to find different ways to jack up the price. This one doesn't make a whole lotta sense. The ratings go from D to Z (apparently A, B and C were on holidays). The less colour a diamond has, the rarer, better and more expensive it is. Unless it has a nice colour—like red, pink, blue or green—then it's even rarer, better and more expensive. These are called 'fancy' diamonds. The short of it is: colour bad, unless it's pretty, then colour good.

Putting 'fancy' diamonds aside (God help you if your bride just has to have a pink diamond like her cousin Sherry's), you're probably looking at diamonds in the G to J 'Near Colourless' range. The D to F 'Colourless' range is very rare and extremely pricey, while anything below J is probably not going to cut the mustard for an engagement ring (it may even have a mustard hue).

THE FIFTH C—BLOODY *COST*

Some wedding books (even those allegedly written for men) suggest that it's all right to spare no expense when it comes to the ring. That's wrong and irresponsible. What is an appropriate budget for the engagement ring? The common refrain is two months' salary (sometimes you hear three). Whether that means before or after tax is anyone's guess, but unfortunately love is not tax deductible (though the Greens might push that through). In any event, the two months rule is entirely suspect, created as it was by the diamond industry (a DeBeers marketing campaign from the 1940s). Fortunately, I've never heard of a woman responding to a proposal by asking: 'What portion of your salary does this ring represent, and is that net or gross?' If you get that response then you might need to shop around some more, but not for a ring.

When budgeting for a ring, you need to consider your personal financial circumstances and factor in the costs of the wedding, the honeymoon and the life that you and your partner are starting together (a house, children, etc.). *Think very carefully before wiping out your savings or, worse, going into debt for a ring.* It's more important to be a responsible husband than a lavish groom. You can start with a modest ring and give your wife a more extravagant one at a future anniversary, once you've landed that buyout offer from Google and have the scratch.

Romance is not about money. Romance is about how well you know the woman you want to marry and how much time, effort and thought you put into a choice as personal and enduring as her engagement ring. Of course, you may know that the woman you want to marry wants the biggest damn rock anyone has ever seen, in which case romance is gonna mug you like an unemployed ice addict.

A ring can have special meaning to your partner in several ways. You could include her birthstone. If she's proud of her Spanish heritage, seek out a Spanish design for the ring. She may have had a special connection with her grandmother, so you could recreate her grandmother's engagement ring, lost to the family years ago, from pictures. Another possibility is a family ring of your own.

ANTIQUE VS CASH CONVERTERS

Leading the parade of wedding absurdities is the difference between two types of *used* engagement rings. It's more proof that money tends to be the deciding factor on romance, according to the powers that be.

	ANTIQUE	CASH CONVERTERS
Degree of Usedness	Very Used to Very, Very Used	Slightly to Somewhat Used
Expense	$$$$$	$
Reaction	Romantic	Cheap Bastard

A ring bought in a pawn shop may be significantly cheaper than a new ring, but pray she never finds the receipt. However, other *used* rings are renamed 'antique' and sold at a big mark-up. What's the real difference between 'second-hand' and 'antique'? I have no earthly idea, but I can provide some general guidelines. If it's a ten-year-old ring sold by a recent divorcee looking to score some black market anti-depressants, then it's second-hand. If it's a 200-year-old ring once belonging to Dame Frumpy Britches, then it's an antique.

HEIRLOOMS

Valuable or not, a family ring can be very romantic, especially if it has a great story behind it. The ring I gave my wife has a unique art deco design and my grandfather won it in a poker game while serving in World War II (sadly, his poker skills must have skipped my generation as I'm hopeless). An heirloom ring forms an immediate bond between your bride and your family. It's also more likely to be unique and not a ring that anyone could get at the shop. And as far as the Fifth C is concerned, an heirloom ring is two months' salary for the unemployed man.

Of course, she may not like the ring. In fact, she may hate it. She may wear it like a crushing burden for the sake of your love and your family's acceptance and, as with Frodo in *The Lord of the Rings*, it will slowly poison her soul against you until her reservoir of resentment spills over and she lashes out at you for no reason. Of course, that's a worst-case scenario.

Ah, but I have a cunning plan (one that worked for me):

1. Propose with the heirloom ring and tell your girlfriend that you want her to have the ring she wants (one which she picks out), but you also wanted to have a ring to hand her when you proposed.

2. Tell your girlfriend the history of the ring and its meaning to your family. She may love the family ring and its history and want to keep it (particularly if family, friends and colleagues pay big compliments). If not, then it's time to shop, but you're no worse off than you were before.

3. To avoid family disappointment, tell them that *you are only using the ring to propose* and that you will likely be getting a different ring in the end. Don't put your bride in the position of *rejecting* the family heirloom and potentially slighting your family. If your partner decides to keep the ring, it will be a pleasant surprise for your family (unless someone harboured a secret desire for the ring, but that's their tough luck).

RESIZING VS RESETTING

Resizing of a family ring is a given, but be careful about a complete resetting (taking a valuable stone or stones and putting them into a newly designed ring). It could offend your family, so check first and don't presume.

THE RING BEARER

It's traditional to propose with a ring, like in the movies. She says 'yes' and you slip it on her finger. It completes the moment. On the other hand, many men worry that she won't like the ring they pick (like when Frodo gives Cate Blanchett his ring, and she turns into a fiery dark witch). So, some men shop for the ring afterwards *with* their partner—a logical move. There's no right way to go about it, but if you plan to buy the ring beforehand you can take some steps to ensure it's a ring she'll love. Research, investigation, listening and consultation are key.

1. *Research.* Research diamonds, other gems and settings. There's plenty of useful information on the net. Also, take a look at any jewellery your partner already has, to get a sense of her style.

2. *Investigation.* Check out a couple of jewellers, beginning with personal recommendations from friends or relatives who got married recently or who regularly buy jewellery.

3. *Listening.* Pay attention to any hints your girlfriend drops, like rings she's pointed out in windows or rings on other women that she's liked, loved or hated. Hint dropping is how she gets what she wants, while maintaining the illusion that it's your brilliant idea. Of course, some women provide pictures or physically point out the ring they want, in which case there you go (if you can afford it).

4. *Consultation.* Consult with her sister or best friend— whoever's most likely to be her maid of honour. Women talk to other women about stuff, including the ring they want. Just don't let the circle get too wide, otherwise word of your impending proposal will leak out. Make sure it's someone who knows

your partner's tastes and is capable of keeping a secret, but don't expect her to hold out forever. You can ask your adviser for general pointers, take her along when you check out jewellers, ask for her thoughts on your final choices or just ask her to confirm your pick.

Point of No Return

As a general rule, jewellers will not accept a returned engagement ring, though you should check your jeweller's policy. If you have a good relationship with them, they might offer to try selling it to someone else and give you what they get for it. Otherwise, your options are pretty slim. You can sell it on eBay or, for a 'name' designer ring, take it to a reputable auctioneer or antique dealer. Otherwise, it's off to the pawn shop, or you can sell the ring for scrap, but you'll get less than the market rate in either case. In short, *make sure you get it right*.

INTERPRETING HINTS

Women have a way of talking about other stuff when they're really talking about your stuff. She probably won't say: 'I want a simple, diamond engagement ring with four prongs and a platinum band.' She might say: 'Did you see Debbie's engagement ring? It was so showy and it was yellow gold, which is *so* last century. I think simple rings are better, with a quality diamond and platinum for durability, like Rebecca's ring.' Neither you nor she came up in that statement and she didn't actually tell you what kind of ring she wanted . . . and yet, *she just told you what kind of ring she wanted.*

SHOPPING WITH HER

If you're shopping with your partner for the engagement ring, some of your problems are solved. You don't have to worry about picking a ring she won't like. You can also count on her for some knowledge of diamonds and rings, though it's still good to have a rough idea about quality and cost yourself (you don't throw down thousands on a car without checking under the hood). It will also impress your new bride when you unexpectedly drop some diamond knowledge on her.

Your major difficulty is *her* expectations dramatically exceeding *your* budget. Some wedding books recommend speaking with jewellers ahead of time about your budget, so your partner is only shown rings in your price range. Nice idea, but if those rings don't measure up your partner is going to ask to see others, and who is the jeweller to say no when it's in the jeweller's interest to say yes?

It's very, very difficult not to buy the love of your life the ring she really wants. However, getting married is about the long term. While the groom usually pays for the ring, this is more symbolism than reality. The two of you are going to pool your resources in the marriage, and the less money *you* bring in the less money the two of you will have as a married couple. If your budget isn't measuring up for her, explain how and why you set it: you had to take account of wedding costs, the honeymoon and things that you both want for your future together. If your partner is entering into a lifetime commitment, she should recognise the importance of those things too.

IT'S SETTING IN NOW

Relative to the diamond, the ring setting will be a fraction of the ring's total cost. That said, the price of gold and other precious metals ain't cheap. In terms of style, yellow gold is less in favour these days, but fashion is fickle so check out the store windows and ask someone who knows about these things (i.e., a woman). Platinum is generally the preferred choice and the most expensive. If you can't afford platinum, white gold is a close proximity and might even look better, depending on the stone and individual taste.

Style is a personal thing, so check your girlfriend's jewellery stash to see whether she has more items in yellow gold or in lighter coloured metals (silver, white gold, platinum). Also, ask her sister or a trusted friend about her tastes. This can go beyond the choice of metal to other aspects of style. Does she like modern jewellery, a classical style, art deco or art nouveau? Don't know what those things mean? That's okay, the jeweller will, so you can just ask to see things in your partner's preferred style.

STONED AGAIN

Diamond is the traditional and simplest choice of stones, but not the only option. Some women don't even like diamonds, and if that's true about your girlfriend you probably know it (lucky bastard). So, you might be looking at a sapphire, emerald, pearl or ruby ring, or a ring with no stone at all. Birthstones are a common alternative, though you're out of luck if, like me, your special lady was born in April (yep, it's diamond). Unfortunately, I have neither the time, knowledge nor publishing space to get into the particulars of other precious stones. Go use the internet—it's not just for porn.

Of course, your partner may want a diamond *and* another stone (poor bastard), in which case you'll just have to allocate your resources accordingly. For example, diamond and blue sapphire is a popular combination. As a tip, a bunch of small stones is not too expensive compared to a single large stone. If you want to add some sparkle to the ring without totally blowing your budget, include some small diamonds or other small stones to set off the main stone. A row of small diamonds embedded in a woman's engagement ring or the wedding band is becoming popular.

WEDDING BANDS

Wedding bands tend to be much more straightforward, as you're generally not dealing with stones (at least, not large ones). Also, this is something you'll choose *with* your partner, and will be part of your overall wedding budget. The other major difference is that one of these rings is meant for *you*. For most men, the wedding band will be the first and only piece of jewellery they will ever wear, and it's meant to be with you for life. So give it some consideration. You want something comfortable that you don't mind looking at.

Gold is especially pricey these days, so even a simple gold band can be expensive. Platinum is even more expensive. If you're really not interested in spending a lot on your ring, or you're afraid that you'll lose it, you can go with a titanium band. They are very light, durable and a plain band runs about $200. Another option is palladium, which sounds made up but is a sturdy, blended metal that includes some white gold and has a similar look. It will cost considerably more than a titanium band, but less than gold.

If you want a ring that means something to you, there are ways to personalise it. An inscription is the simplest. You can use the date of your wedding (a good anniversary reminder) or a message from your bride, with a similar inscription in her band. You can also look for ring designs that reflect your ethnic, religious or family history. I'm from America but have an Irish background, so I reached back to my Irish heritage and chose a Celtic ring design. There may also be ways to incorporate a family crest or similar emblem into your ring.

Super Size

Most rings can be resized relatively easily, but rings with a particular design (like my Celtic band) and titanium rings cannot be. I'm sure you plan to keep yourself in shape but, as time passes, you will not be the same lithe lad of today. Your fingers *will* swell. I see guys in their forties and fifties and it looks like their wedding band is strangling their fourth finger—I'm just waiting for the thing to turn gangrenous and fall off.

I built a half size of room into my ring, to grow into. It also makes it easier to get over the knuckle. The more traditional among you may never take off the ring, but I find that impractical. I take it off when I work out and whenever I go swimming or to the beach. It's a miracle I haven't lost the thing yet, but the prospect of my wife's wrath keeps me in check.

Actually, I did *misplace* my ring once. I was about to buy a plain, titanium replacement, because I 'can't be trusted with nice things'. Thankfully, the original turned up, wedged between some towels in the linen cupboard. I have one friend, though, who's on his third ring now—all titanium, so at least he knows himself.

The Power of the Ring

Don't be surprised if certain women take a greater interest in you once you're married, but stick a pin in that ego 'cause *it's all about the ring*. It symbolises your value to women because it means you're valued by a woman *and* it signals your complete unavailability. That's a powerful pheromone cocktail. I didn't believe this myself until the very first night after my wedding, when I went up to the bar to get a beer.

The first thing I noticed was an attractive blonde checking me out. Then a brunette on my left started chatting to me. Now, I had reasonable success with women in my single days, but I can count on one finger the times attractive women came up to *me* at a bar to start a conversation.

But, remember this and remember it well: some women are nutjobs. You know this, because you dated enough of them in your single days. One

MORE ON NUTJOBS

Sorry, ladies, but I stand by my nutjob comments, though it's not necessarily a permanent condition. Some women go through nutjob phases, when they're *only* interested in unavailable men, and then snap out of it. It's like Sally's friend (Carrie Fisher) in *When Harry Met Sally*, who kept dating married men until she meets a nice writer, settles down and gives up her nutjobbery.

great thing about getting married—no more dating nutjobs. And if a woman is drawn to you *because* you're engaged or married, then she is, by definition, a nutjob. So, if you end up with boiled bunnies in your kitchen, the shadow of a carving knife creeping up your shower curtain or your political career in tatters, don't come crying to me. You were warned. Nutjobs.

3

YOUR BRIDE AND YOU

Inside the Mind of Your Bride

*'[W]e are getting married, and yet it seems like
I'm the only one who cares about the details of the
day . . . Raphael . . . says that he's happy to help if I tell
him what I want him to do. But I don't want to have to
tell him what to do, I want him to come to me with ideas
and excitement about the wedding'*
(quoted in Paul 2000, p. 112).

. . . She wants you to *want* to do the dishes.

THE DISHES PRINCIPLE

The dishes principle is ably depicted in a scene between Brooke (Jennifer Aniston) and Gary (Vince Vaughn) in *The Break-up*:

> Gary: Fine, I'll help you do the damn dishes.
>
> Brooke: Oh, come on. You know what? No, see, that's not what I want.
>
> Gary: You just said that you want me to help you do the dishes.
>
> Brooke: I want you to *want* to do the dishes.
>
> Gary: Why would I want to do dishes? Why?
>
> Brooke: See, that's my whole point.

The problem is, weddings just aren't our bag, baby. Men don't know much about weddings going in, nor do they have much interest in the various aspects of weddings. But if you meet your bride halfway by showing a willingness to help, she should provide you with a little direction instead of getting upset because you're not coming to her 'with ideas and excitement'. In order to reach that happy truce, you'll need some understanding of what's going on in your bride's mind as well as the reality of her wedding-induced stress.

BRIDAL PSYCHOLOGY: OVERVIEW

The female mind is a mysterious place, and many men have lost themselves in its labyrinthine passages. I cannot promise you a way out, but hopefully I can give you a view from above. For that, you have to know a little about where your bride is coming from and the unique aspects of her wedding stress. We can start with something my bride said to me one stressful day (after a few cocktails). I think it sums things up pretty perfectly: 'I just want to stand up in front of our family and friends and tell them how much I love you. It should be that simple . . . and when it's not, I get frustrated.'

Why Your Bride Loses It

The term 'bridezilla' may once have been clever, but it has become all too clichéd. Bridezilla—something now typified in our culture by a proliferation of insipid reality-TV programming—suggests that your loving, patient, considerate girlfriend is somehow transformed into a self-obsessed wedding demon by an unexplained force, like the gamma rays that turn Bruce Banner into the Incredible Hulk. It's important for you to understand that there are *reasons* why women go a little insane during the wedding planning (and yes, one of them may be you).

First and foremost, weddings are incredibly massive, complex, expensive and difficult events to organise. That's why there's a profession that exists to do just that (wedding planners). Think of it: what your partner is trying to do in her spare time is what someone else does for a living. If you're not very involved in the planning of your wedding, pick up your partner's wedding folder and flip through it or grab a traditional wedding book and look at the to-do lists or budget page. This will give you a sense of what a huge undertaking this is.

Yes, your partner may become irritable, short-tempered, anxious, aggressive and moody. She may lose her sense of humour and, at times, seem like an entirely different person from the woman you fell in love with. Yet this is not a unique transformation. I know many women *and men* who suffer similar symptoms when working long and hard hours on a legal case, a political campaign or other stressful work projects. Except your bride doesn't have the support of a team of work colleagues. She mostly has you and, when you think about how much help you are, that ain't much. Add to that the stresses that come from dealing with family and trying to make everyone happy.

So, when you and your partner find yourselves in various prickly moments, it's best to cut her some slack. Your life will be much better if you do and much worse if you don't. You can also help relieve her stress by doing some of the following:

1. *Treatment.* Get her a massage (you can even join her) or a day at the spa.
2. *Do something.* Take some wedding chores off her hands. You may have to pry things away from her (more about that below), but do it.
3. *Break time.* Make her take a break from all things wedding, whether it's a scheduled day each week (like a date night) or something less formal.
4. *Unexpected gift.* As Sean Connery said in *Finding Forrester*: 'The key to a woman's heart is an unexpected gift at an unexpected time.' It doesn't have to be anything major. Even a small gift goes a long way when it comes without any obligation to give it (like a birthday or anniversary).

Wedding Dress

My wife is not an overly emotional person, but she came back one day from wedding dress shopping practically in tears. What's so hard about shopping for a dress? I thought it was supposed to be fun? Let's run through what I didn't understand.

She spends the day trying on dresses, few of which fit because she's a woman (she has hips and a bust) and the dresses are designed for models (seventeen-year-old girls built like twelve-year-old boys). So, she spends the day being poked, prodded and tucked in ways that makes her feel every perceived flaw in her body keenly. She's told outright by salesgirls that she looks terrible in some of the dresses (bear in mind that women are deeply emotionally invested in looking beautiful on their wedding day). Other salesgirls look at her as if she can't afford anything in their store and treat her like she's wasting their time. At other shops she's made to feel bad because she isn't willing to spend more. Some stores won't even talk to her, because they need at least *six months* to tailor the dress and she's left it too late (or they'll charge 20 per cent extra for the 'rush job'). That was just one day. It brings me to tears just to write about it.

Then, after a day being made to feel like crap, she comes home to pour out her troubles to her loving partner and he says that she's just being 'silly—it's just dress shopping, how hard can it be?' The truth is, we have no idea, and we never will. The wedding dress is just one example, but we *assume* it's all easy. When our bride gets upset, we tell ourselves she's being irrational or acting like a 'bridezilla'. Instead, don't assume anything. If your bride is upset, listen to her for a bit. Sometimes that's all she needs. And if she's spent the day feeling less than pretty, tell her she's beautiful. She'll say, 'You're just saying that,' but she still wants to hear it.

Bride's Mood on the Day

According to *The Conscious Bride* (which I like to refer to as *The Unconscious Bride*), on the wedding day your bride may be 'moving from chaos to serenity and presence, and from serenity back to chaos and absence' (Paul 2000, p. 144). That sounds like a lot of transport costs, but she won't need a limo—it's a *metaphorical journey.* The truth is, most brides are happy and joyous on their wedding day. If not, it's usually because they let their expectations get so out of control that any minor deviation from the plan is perceived as an unmitigated disaster.

Putting Down the Veil

Moving on from the wedding isn't much of an issue for men. I once asked a recently married friend what life was like, post-wedding. He said it was like it was before they got married, but better, because they didn't have to deal with wedding planning any more. I thought the exact same thing after our wedding (well, once we got those damn thankyou notes done). Again, I refer to *The Conscious Bride*: 'Men . . . tend to swashbuckle their way through the vines and tumbleweeds of their emotional terrain' (Paul 2000, p. 177). An impressive statement, not for the analysis but for the tortuous mix of pirate, Tarzan and western metaphors.

For brides, there's been so much planning and build-up to the wedding that a certain amount of let-down is inevitable. More importantly, it's a day when the bride is the unequivocal centre of attention, and that's ended now. As my wife put it, 'It wasn't all about me any more,' and it's hard to come down from that pedestal. That said, some brides really go off the deep end, such as a woman described in *The Smart Couple's Guide*: 'Each day for a month, she put on her wedding gown and wandered around the house, looking at herself in the mirror' (Shervan and Sniechowski 2005, p. 206). Another bride sat on the bed crying for hours *on her wedding night*, refusing to take off her dress (pp. 206–7). So, how do you prevent your bride from turning into a crazy lady?

These extreme reactions are a symptom of seeing the wedding only as an end in itself, and not as the beginning of a marriage. During the wedding planning, don't just take breaks from wedding talk. Make time for talking about your lives *after* the wedding. Talk about children, buying a house, where you want to live, where your careers are heading and trips you want to take. Try to create a beachhead for your bride in the post-wedding world, so she has a place to land when the wedding ride lets off.

MRS JEKYLL AND MRS HYDE

Before delving into traditional groom duties and other ways you might involve yourself in the wedding planning in the next chapter, you have to know what your bride expects of you. In short: (i) you are to be an enthusiastic partner in the planning, and (ii) she is the only one who knows how to do things the *right way* and you are an idiot. Meet Mrs Jekyll and Mrs Hyde.

Mrs Jekyll . . .

Many things about weddings make men uncomfortable, much like being in the feminine hygiene section of the chemist. We tend to focus on *getting married* and the *marriage* and get frustrated when the wedding gets in the way of the important things. Why is it such a big deal that you don't care about the colour scheme, or the choice of flowers, or who sits where, or who does what? The problem is, in your partner's mind your lack of interest in these seeming trivialities is actually bound up with all the important things, which is how you get this tripe: 'He's not actively helping with the wedding because it's not as important to him, so I must not be as important to him as he is to me' (Paul 2000, p. 114). So, because you're not interested in the minutiae of the wedding, your bride thinks you're not excited about her or getting married to her when just the opposite is true (irony's a bitch sometimes).

So, what's a man to do? Feign enthusiasm about things that you don't care about, in order to appear enthusiastic about things which you are, in fact, enthusiastic about? That's ridiculous and it makes my head hurt.

. . . and Mrs Hyde

The flip side of the coin is the control freak: a bride who needs to control *everything*. She has way too much on her plate to stay sane, but you have to pry tasks away from her like an impacted molar. And when you do things, they're always completely wrong, because they're not exactly the way she would do them.

Here's the real killer. These contradictory personalities—Mrs Jekyll and Mrs Hyde—frequently coexist in the *same bride*. One moment you'll be chastised for not helping (or not wanting to help) and the next you'll be berated for 'doing it all wrong'.

Working with Mrs Jekyll

When you get hit with the 'you don't love me because you don't care about the flower arrangements' bit, you *could* respond with the following points about wedding details:

1. They involve a whole lot of things (table settings, flowers, dresses, sappy music, group dancing, etc.) that simply aren't your game.
2. They often overwhelm what is most important, namely love, marriage and a new life together. So, your allegedly callous indifference is actually a reflection of your greater emotional depth. So there.

It may not go down very well, but you'll have the satisfaction of being right. Of course, as any married man can tell you, that satisfaction is a fleeting joy sacrificed on the altar of much pain and suffering. So, keep these points between us, and instead try to show some *interest*, if not enthusiasm, and a desire to be helpful. If you can't come to her with 'ideas and excitement', come to her with questions. Men need a place to start with weddings and questions show some interest without the need to offer up anything specific. Then, listen to her and offer to help out on the bits and pieces where you think you can be useful. Once your partner provides some general parameters and direction, you might even find that you have some ideas depending on the subject.

Working with Mrs Hyde

My bride was stressed one day about all the things she had to do for the wedding, and when I asked if I could help she insisted there was nothing I could do. So, I asked her to take out her to-do list and I immediately picked off several items. It was nothing much (a few phone calls, emails, tracking some things down), but it took a few things off her plate, reduced her stress and established the following principles: (i) she did not have to do everything herself, and (ii) I was not completely useless. If your stressed bride insists that 'there's nothing you can do', ask her, calmly, if she can show you her to-do list (she will have a list, folder, spreadsheet or, in some cases, an entire book). Go through it with her and I'm sure you'll find a few things you can handle. She isn't the only person who can confirm a car reservation. Get instructions, as detailed as necessary. As you complete things, let her know so she can cross them off her list. Then that throbbing in her neck vein might slow to a nice reggae rhythm.

TARZAN AND JANE

Tarzan was not opposed to being involved in the wedding planning, but every jungle man has his limits. As Tarzan put it, when confronted with seemingly insignificant wedding detail number 4392, something in him snapped and the following conversation took place:

Tarzan: Okay, let's begin by assuming that I *care* about this wedding detail which, of course, I don't. But let's say that I do. Then let's say that there's a choice between Option A and Option B for this detail. You ask me my opinion and I want Option A, but it turns out that you want Option B. On the day of the wedding, what's it going to be? Option A or Option B?

Jane: Option B.

Tarzan: Then what in the hell is the point of this conversation? You are asking me about things I don't care about, and if I have an opinion different from yours IT WON'T MATTER!

Tarzan's advice: Don't say anything remotely like this. It did not go over well.

COMMUNICATION

It's important to apply the lessons above to communications with your bride. Say that your partner asks you what you think about the invitations and you say, completely honestly, 'I don't really care about that stuff, baby, whatever you want is fine.' You've given her free rein to do what she wants, which is all you ever want for the decisions *you* care about, like choosing home entertainment equipment. She should be happy, but instead all she hears is that *you don't care*. In her mind, *not caring* about the invitations means you don't care about the wedding, her friends and family, her happiness or your lives together. If she tries to explain this to you, you might say: 'But that's ridiculous, of course I care about those things.' Now you've just called her ridiculous and told her that she's wrong to feel the way she's feeling. Grab a blanket, have fun on the couch and enjoy all the not having sex.

What you have to appreciate is that you may say one thing to your bride, but she may hear something completely different. You have two choices. You can say that she's in the wrong: you say what you mean, and if she reads something else into it that's her fault, not yours. You can also stand on a cliff and yell at the wind to blow in the other direction. Alternatively, you can accept that men and women communicate differently and try to learn how she hears what you say. Then apply that to your conversations on wedding details. Here are a few examples of innocent things you might say and the translation to what she hears:

Example 1: Various Wedding Details

Groom says: I don't know, baby. Women are usually better at flowers and colours and stuff. Why don't you handle it?

Bride hears: Women are also better at cooking, cleaning and changing nappies, and you can expect me to do none of these things in our life together.

Example 2: Mother of the Bride

Groom says: I really have no idea what your mother should wear for the ceremony.

Bride hears: It's not that I don't like your mother, it's just that she means nothing to me.

Example 3: Bridesmaids

Groom says: I think your cousin would look really good in that bridesmaid dress.

Bride hears: I want to have sex with your cousin.

Unfortunately, there's no comprehensive groom-to-bride dictionary and no language courses on offer at the nation's academic institutions. Just try to remember that complete lack of interest is bad, and that if your partner is stressed, annoyed or upset with you for other reasons (which, of course, she will not tell you about) then you can be sure that anything you say will be given the worst possible interpretation.

HELPFUL READING

If you and your partner are constantly fighting over miscommunications, I recommend the book *You Just Don't Understand Me* by Deborah Tannen. I know men usually avoid relationship books like the plague, for good reason, but this one has merit. First, Tannen has a PhD in linguistics. It's not like the guy who spent nine years as a monk and then sat down to write *Men are from Mars, Women are from Venus*. Second, Tannen doesn't blame men for the miscommunications; rather, by making both sides aware of the different ways they communicate, she minimises the misunderstandings.

DELEGATING tasks to His groomsmen had gone well, but perhaps He should have chosen the suit himself...

4

GROOM DUTIES AND WEDDING CHORES

Things You Need to Pretend to Care About

'A groom doesn't have to be involved in a specific decision
to be an active, supportive part of the planning process.
Often, he can be helpful simply by joining his future
bride on her errands'
(Post 2006, p. 65).

. . . I know—what a comfort.

There are so many little, tiny, damn details involved in a wedding. In the words of Will Ferrell in *Blades of Glory*, it's 'mind-bottling' ('. . . when things are all crazy and it's like your mind is trapped in a bottle'). While these details are mostly unfathomable to you, by some biological miracle your partner has an uncanny ability to consider them all at once. They spew forth from her in incredible volume and detail, but it's too much information for your primitive male mind to process. Then she sees in your eyes the 'not responding' signal that appears whenever you use a Microsoft product.

To avoid the forthcoming dust-up, let's try to break off some manageable pieces of the wedding pie for you. First off, few men even know what grooms *traditionally* do (yes, there's more than just proposing and showing up—there's *looking good* too). Moreover, things have changed since the 1500s, so your partner may want to involve herself in some of the traditional groom areas (like honeymoon planning) and unfortunately, she may want to involve *you* in the million and one things that the bride or her family traditionally looked after. Among those, there may be some things that you're better equipped and more willing to do than others.

TRADITIONAL GROOM DUTIES

The traditional duties of a groom can vary by country and tradition, but the following list provides a broad overview. Most of these duties are discussed in greater detail in other chapters (cross-references noted).

1. Proposing (Chapter 1).
2. Selecting and paying for an engagement ring (Chapter 2).

3. Choosing the best man and groomsmen, and making sure they know what they're doing (Chapter 10).

4. Choosing your wedding outfit (discussed below) and those of the groomsmen (Chapter 10), though your bride may want some say in both.

5. Anything else to do with the groomsmen, like thank-you gifts, arranging for lodging, etc. (Chapter 10).

6. Pulling together your side of the guest list, including liaising with your parents and family (Chapter 5).

7. Booking wedding night accommodation. If you're having the reception at a hotel, or many of your guests are staying at a particular hotel, then you'll likely stay there as you may get the room gratis or at a discount.

8. Arranging for transportation getting you, your bride and the wedding party to the ceremony, reception and back (Chapter 7).

9. Handling official paperwork, formalities and legalities, like your marriage certificate and registration. You need to check and manage the deadlines, as different states and countries have different rules (i.e., you may have to submit a particular form a day, week or month before your wedding). Your officiant should be able to guide you through the process and requirements in your area.

10. Paying the preacher and making any other wedding day payments (the band, gratuities, etc.). These days, most payments are made in advance by credit card or bank transfer, but you may have a few payments to make on the day itself. As you don't want any hassle

then, prepare the payments ahead of time and give them to the best man to hand over to the relevant people (Chapter 10).

11. Surviving your bucks' night, which is mostly organised by your best man, with some input from you (Chapter 13).

12. Planning the honeymoon, though brides are involving themselves in that more often (chapter 16). This includes making sure everything is in order, particularly for overseas trips (such as passports, visas, shots, travel insurance and snake-bite kit).

13. Getting dressed, showing up and looking dashing (Chapter 15).

14. The groom's toast—well, who else would do it? (Chapter 14).

DON'T HESITATE TO DELEGATE

When I got engaged, a friend made me an offer that a friend of his had once made to him: if there was something that I forgot about or didn't have time for, I could call on him for help. Unless you're a complete prick, I'm sure you'll have a few friends willing to lend a hand, starting with your groomsmen (Chapter 10 discusses specific ways they can help). Don't overburden any single person or delegate all your responsibilities (then you *will* be a prick), and some of your duties are nondelegable, like proposing (you can't ask a mate to tell your bride that you '*like* her like her'). Lastly, to ensure the karmic wedding flow, be sure to help your mates when their time comes.

THINGS YOU MAY WANT TO DO MORE THAN OTHER THINGS

The traditional groom duties are a useful baseline, as they tend to fall in the male comfort zone (as opposed to flower arrangements or invitation design). Still, you and your bride can divide wedding tasks however you like. The important thing is that *you do your bit*, so your bride doesn't go insane or come to hate you. There are a number of other ways you might want to contribute as well.

Tunes, Pics and Research

If you're a former member of the A/V club (no shame), you can organise the photographer and video guy. Music junkies can arrange for the music, whether it be a band, DJ or your own iPod (all discussed in Chapter 7). You can also do research on anything, like venues, caterers and hotels. Any guy can make a few phone calls or search the net to get information on costs and availability. You may even start having 'ideas' (though 'excitement' is still a stretch). Just make sure you get some guidelines from your bride before going off half-cocked. There's no sense checking costs on a German beer hall when she's looking for a seaside, historic mansion.

Webbing Your Wedding

If you're a tech-savvy blogging king or just familiar with Facebook, then you can set up a website for your wedding. Couples are increasingly using websites to communicate with their guests. They allow you to provide a lot more information than can be crammed into an invitation, as well as update guests with new details or changes. You can include directions, hotel information, a link to your gift registry, tips on things to see and do in the area, information about subsidiary events (like a day-after brunch) and anything else. You don't have to be a web expert or fluent with HTML. There are several online services that provide relatively easy to use templates for setting up your wedding website (for a fee, of course). We used www.wedding window.com, which was quite good and seems to get the highest recommendations, but Google 'wedding websites' to see the various options. It's also probably worth a few extra dollars to get a short, easy to remember web address for your site, like www.bobandjanewedding. com. Some of the wedding websites can set that up, for an additional fee, or you can buy your own web address separately and redirect it to your wedding website. Otherwise, just imagine including this URL on your prim and proper wedding invitation: http:// www.weddingwindow.com/Bob-Jane/wedding/href8sept/ randomtechjargon.html.

> **DIGNITY ON THE WEB**
> Like all things wedding, websites have the potential to go over the top, with gaggingly cute features like asking friends and family to send inspirational messages or telling the sappy tale of how your relationship 'blossomed'. All the more reason for you to take on the website task—to keep your dignity among your mates.

TIPS FOR WEDDING CHORES

When you're called upon to go with your partner to choose the wedding invitations, the flowers or, God forbid, the bridesmaid dresses, it's important to remember a few things.

She May Hate This Too

Don't assume that your partner is loving all this—it may be a chore for her too. Even the most eager, fairytale-loving, pink-bow-wearing bride-to-be can get buried in the avalanche of wedding details. She may want you along not 'to share in the magic of the moment', as the wedding books say, but to provide some support when she's wedding weary.

Don't Go Cranky, Sleepy, Hungry (or Any of the Other Dwarves)

My partner and I have found that we both get cranky when we're hungry, tired or hung-over, and that being cranky is the major source of our disagreements. So, before heading to the stationers for a three-hour consideration of the shape, colour and design of your invitations, make sure that neither of you are in any such depleted condition. It was pushing two o'clock when my bride and I got to the invitation joint one day, and neither of us had eaten lunch. I told her that we better pop over to the cafe across the street first, or it would all end in tears. Just be sure to make it a light meal to avoid the food coma effect.

Don't Drink and Bride

A few quiet ales to relax is not a bad idea, but it's a very slippery slope. The Elvis impersonator may have seemed

> **BATTLE OF BRISBANE**
>
> In 1942 Brisbane was a garrison city, headquarters of General Douglas MacArthur and home to tens of thousands of American and Australian servicemen. On 26 and 27 November tensions over the privileged position of American GIs, who were 'over paid, oversexed and over here', advanced from brawls to outright riot. In the end, an Australian serviceman was shot and killed and scores of American and Australian soldiers were sent to hospital. And it was all set off when an Aussie digger called American beer 'piss weak'.

like a good musical choice while under the influence, but not in the harsh light of day. Alcohol has also been known to lead to disagreements between would-be partners.

Don't Fight Over Nothing

It's possible to care too much. As men, we tend to argue for the sake of arguing. So, you may find yourself in the flower shop, choking back the hay fever during an all-out screaming match over the merits of petunias over chrysanthemums. Just remember that you didn't know what those things were a few weeks ago and couldn't give a rat's arse which of them get hung by the pews on your wedding day. Concede the point, then go back to the pub where you belong.

Follow a Question with a Question

If you just don't care about some particular wedding detail, try to show some semblance of interest anyway. A good approach is to follow her question with a question. There's a bit of an art to this. For instance, you can't always say,

'I don't know, what do you think?' or simply repeat her question back to her. She'll see through that. So, if your bride asks you which of the flower arrangements you prefer, say, 'It's a difficult choice—which do you like most?' It may not be a diffi-cult choice, but she's not really looking for your opinion. As noted in Chapter 3 she's already formed an opinion, which will be the ultimate decision. Your question just shows a small amount of interest, which is all she really wanted from you.

> **THE INTERROGATION**
>
> Watch out, because your partner may follow up your questions with more questions, for example: 'I like these three arrangements—which do you prefer?' You can try responding with another question, but she may want to pin you down on a real opinion or she may have caught on to the questions bit. If you have to make a call, *don't panic*. Remember, your advantage is that you don't really care, so pick any of them. If she asks you why you picked *that* one, I've got nothing for you. You may want to give up and marry someone else.

'A Man's Got to Know His Limitations'

Dirty Harry was right. There's only so much a man can take, and it's important to be aware of your limitations. If you can't stand to hear one more word about bows, bouton-nieres and bonbonnières without exploding into a rant, then walk it off. Take deep breaths, have a beer, go surfing, whatever. Talk to a mate who's recently gone through the process to get it off your chest (a neat women's trick, but it works for blokes too). If you're unable to get away at the moment (e.g., you're stuck at a lunch with your future bride,

HAPPY'S HAPPY PLACE

In *Happy Gilmore*, starring Adam Sandler in the title role, Happy's 'happy place' featured his love interest dressed in sexy lingerie holding two jugs of beer, his grandma winning at the pokies and a dwarf in a cowboy outfit riding around on a wooden hobbyhorse. So, go for your life.

mother-in-law and sister-in-law), then try to put yourself into a mental happy place by planning your bucks' night or replaying the most recent footy match in your head.

If you're truly desperate, try explaining to your bride, in a calm and conciliatory way, that you're getting overwhelmed by the volume of details. However, this should not be done in the presence of other company, because there's a risk you might end up copping a rant yourself about how you have no idea about all the details, and how she has to deal with everything, and how you're doing so little and on and on until your ears bleed.

THEMES AND SCHEMES

One growing trend is to have a 'theme' for the wedding (which cuts against a *theme* of this book: don't do anything for your wedding that's done for a child's birthday party). The theme could relate to anything, like a favourite city or film, a particular era (e.g., Elizabethan or roaring twenties) or a season. The theme can be very abstract and subtle (just determining a colour scheme and style) or it can lead to a full-on costume drama. It might not be a problem, except you can almost guarantee that the theme will have a decidedly feminine bent. So, if your bride is insisting on a dreaded 'theme', try suggesting some of your own. It's a

GROOM VS BRIDE WEDDING THEMES

BRIDE THEME	GROOM THEME
Fairytale/Princess	Western/Cowboy
Flowers	Fishing
An Affair to Remember	*Rocky IV* (the one where he fights the Russian)
Paris	Parramatta
Summer	Cricket
Home and Away	*The Simpsons*

matter of mutually assured destruction. Have a male counter for each of her suggestions for which no compromise is conceivable, and hopefully they'll cancel each other out.

Yes, your wedding is likely to have a colour scheme, which can be determined by your theme. What does this mean? It's like sports teams. Every team has their own colours, so they stand apart on the field when they compete, and the fierceness of wedding competition can match that of any sporting rivalry. My advice is to let your partner pick the colour scheme, as long as you retain veto rights—I don't know how you feel about puce, but you may not want to wear it as a vest.

Our colours were blue and silver, which I was quite happy with because they weren't feminine and were similar to my uni colours. A colour scheme can actually be quite helpful as, for any given wedding feature (flowers, invitations, table settings, bridesmaid dresses), it helps narrow down the dizzying array of options. As you'll discover, anything that helps make decisions easier is like a balm from heaven.

THREADS

> The right suit makes almost as much impact on the day as the bride's dress (Love 2007, p. 64).

Talk about your delusions of grandeur—that's complete bull. The only way your outfit could have as much impact as the bride's dress is in a *bad* way, for being odd, clashing or highly inappropriate. If you're doing your job right, you'll *complement* the bride with a suave and sophisticated ensemble that makes you look dashing. It's a bloody tux or dark suit—it ain't rocket science. For more casual weddings it could be slacks and a blazer, or even a white linen shirt (for a beach wedding). If you want a complete breakdown on what to wear for different levels of formality, the traditional wedding books and websites have all that. The point is, this is *not* the time to get creative.

FEELING BLUE?

In the ultimate bromance, *I Love You, Man*, Peter Klaven (Paul Rudd) managed to pull off a blue tuxedo, but that was a big gamble and it was also a movie (you probably won't have Lou Ferrigno as a groomsman either, but if you do I suppose you can wear *whatever* you want).

Let the Bride be Your Guide

While it may be bad luck for the groom to see the bride's dress before the ceremony, it can be bad luck for the bride *not* to see your threads ahead of time. Even if you think you have good taste in clothes (like me), let your bride, the maid of honour, your sister or a trusted female friend offer some guidance. At the very least, you need to consult with someone who's seen the wedding dress, to make sure you don't clash. Generally, you can assume she'll be on the whitish side of things, and as long as you don't get overly imaginative you should be fine (i.e., for a tux, stick with black, white and shades of silver and grey). Most guys look good in a tux. If you're planning to go off the beaten path, definitely make sure you okay it with your bride first. As a rule, brides don't like surprises.

Fit and Fitting

Make sure what you're wearing fits, or you'll look like a twit and the dancing will be uncomfortable with a too-tight suit. If it's something from your wardrobe, try it on in case all that working out has expanded your chest (or all that beer has expanded your waist). Leave time to get alterations made.

If it's a rental, you'll be fitted when you pick it out, which you should do *months ahead of time*, as the rental shops

NEW SHOES TIP

If you're wearing brand new or rental shoes for the wedding, try to break them in beforehand. When you first put them on, walk around and note any spots where the shoes rub against your foot. Put preventative bandaids on your feet in those spots, and that will keep you from getting sore there or getting blisters, which are no fun on your wedding day.

will run thin on selection and sizes if you leave it too late. Then try it on again a week or two before the wedding, so there's time to make adjustments if your wedding fitness regime made drastic improvements—though rentals usually have adjustment straps on the pants that allow a few centimetres leeway. Lastly, don't choke yourself on the collar— leave some breathing room (literally). It's a collar, not a noose, no matter what your mates say.

Grooming

Among the things that inspired me to write this book were the incredibly condescending grooming suggestions made to grooms in the traditional wedding books—*even those supposedly written by men, for men.* Here are a couple of examples:

From The Groom's Instruction Manual:

Take a shower and clean yourself like you would when preparing for a date . . . Use soap, dumbass, but don't think you need to scrub yourself down until you're red (Fowler 2008, p. 167).

From The Groom's Guide:

Make sure your teeth are really clean and your breath fresh. Have clean hands and clean and trimmed fingernails (Love 2007, p. 80).

As anyone who needs this advice is likely to be illiterate, I don't see the point in putting it in a book. Moreover, I'm going to assume you have more wherewithal than Cletus the slack-jawed yokel from *The Simpsons*, and won't insult you with basic grooming tips.

The only tip I have is to get a haircut a week or so before the wedding, to leave time for it to grow out. Go to your regular barber and stick with your regular cut—this isn't the time to experiment, especially with inventive facial hair. As for *manscaping* (grooming other parts of your man hair), that's getting into fairly personal territory so I'll leave that to you (and your bride).

5

THE LIST

The Big Cull

'Remember that remote cousins often feel as indifferent toward you as you do toward them, and may be happy not to come. The same goes for distant friends'
(www.theknot.com).

. . . If there's one thing you can count on in this world, it's the indifference of family and old friends (for auld lang syne).

The guest list is one of the great wedding stresses. Before you know it, some guy you wouldn't cross the street to piss on if he was on fire is costing you another $120 in food and booze. There are no easy answers, just hard choices, which can be a particular source of tension between the bride, groom and their families.

Does your partner want a large wedding when you want a small one? Do you invite old friends you haven't seen in years or newer friends? Are some of your friends persona non grata with your partner? Do you invite work colleagues (and how do you choose among them)? Are your parents forcing guests on you? No wedding advice can cover all the guest list pitfalls, but I'll give you some of the highlights.

GENERAL PRINCIPLES

Let's start with a few general guest list principles.

Quantity or Quality

Size is one of your first wedding decisions. Are we talking a Rolling Stones crowd or an intimate evening with a lounge act? This is a main factor in your budget (see Chapter 6) and determines the type of interaction you'll have with your guests.

My partner wanted a nicer reception, whereas I cared more about including lots of friends. Fortunately, we weren't far apart on this balance, so we avoided hair-pulling, screaming matches but it was a consistent theme in our 'discussions'. You may find it a major source of strife. If you have very different ideas to your wife on this front then you'll both have to compromise (which mostly means you'll have to give in). In the end our wedding had 86 people, neither intimate nor huge. We had time for brief chats with everyone and a few in-depth talks with our nearest and dearest. Anything much larger and you'll be too busy saying a quick 'hello' to *everyone* to really talk to *anyone*, but that's fine if what really matters to you is that people are there for the event.

If you're determined to have a big wedding but still want quality time with a select few, consider a subsidiary event for your inner circle. Some people use a rehearsal dinner for this purpose (traditionally hosted by the groom's parents), but your catch-up need not be that formal or costly. A picnic or barbecue the day before or after your wedding does the trick. If it's the day before, just choose an activity that won't get you and your mates too loaded.

Don't Wash Your Hands

The guest list is not a task you can fob off on your bride. There are a lot of sensitive politics at play and she won't know the importance of each person on your side (you don't want her dropping the guy who took a bayonet for your dad in 'Nam). So, man up and give her a hand. Also, if the two of you make a tough decision that affects your family, *you* need to handle it. Your bride wants to start out on the right foot with her new in-laws. It's not right to ask her to give your folks the bad news (or the hard word, if it comes to that).

Systematic Approach

It's surprisingly easy to forget someone important when putting together your guest list (sorry, Uncle Floyd). So, to begin, go through all your contacts and think of everyone that you'd ideally like to have at your wedding. This is not your guest list; it's a starting point. You then cull the list down to the number you want.

Beware of Inflation

You have to stick to your target guest number, as painful as that is. If someone else is paying for the wedding, like your bride's parents, it's petty to ask them to spend more so you can expand your list. If you're paying for it yourselves, then you have a budget to maintain and space limitations at your chosen venue. Once you pick a number range many other things fall in place around it, so changing that number later messes with everything. It sucks, but you have to make the hard choices.

The Budget–Guest Balancing Act

I know it's cold, but you'll start seeing people on your guest list as the dollars they'll cost you in food and grog. When working with a budget, you have to balance your numbers against your reception quality. If the guest list is your priority, start there and then consider what type of reception you can afford. If it's important that you serve filet mignon and Penfolds red rather than meat pies and cask wine, then consider the per head cost and determine how many guests get to dig in. No matter your starting point, you'll likely end up making compromises on both sides.

Declines

I know your wedding will be *the* event of the social calendar, but some people will have lame excuses for missing out, like their number coming up on the transplant list. Judging your percentage of declines is a guessing game, which varies from wedding to wedding. Fifteen to 20 per cent is a rough figure to go by, but consider your particular circumstances. If most guests live near the wedding venue, that figure may be lower; if most will have to travel, particularly from overseas, the figure could be higher. As you put your list together, consider the likelihood of attendance for each invitee. There are bound to be some people you are certain will come and others who you are fairly sure won't. That will help you make a better estimate on your final numbers.

(NOT) ALL IN THE FAMILY

Family is what it is, and they have to be the starting point on your guest list. After the immediate family, it can be a harder call. Do you invite *all* the cousins? If you have a lot, you may have to make a call about who's in and who's out. It doesn't seem fair, but it also isn't fair to exclude some of your best friends for the sake of cousins you've seen twice since the Hawke era. So, do what you have to do. If your cousins have barely laid eyes on you in ten years, they probably won't care (and it's a good excuse not to invite you to their wedding). Just be prepared to cop some flak from grumpy uncles, aunts and possibly your parents.

FRIENDS: THE LIST IS YOUR LIFE

When making your guest list, you're effectively choosing the people who will be your friends from now on. As you move forward in life you keep acquiring more friends, until you reach your friend capacity. Then you get into a relationship, which leaves even less time for friends, and you have to make time for *her* friends too. So, in reality, the culling of friends has already begun. The guest list just makes it official. Here are several important friend factors.

Past or Recent Friends

Should you invite more recent friends or very good, old friends? Ask yourself which old friends you have really kept in touch with (and who have kept in touch with you) and prioritise them. If you haven't been in touch with someone in years (Facebook and Twitter don't count, unless you're having a virtual reception), then you may have to resist nostalgia's pull and give them the axe. But have a few representatives from the old days so they can see how hot your wife is.

Long Ago and Far Away

On a related point, you'll naturally feel obliged to invite people to your wedding if you went to theirs. But, if their wedding was more than five years ago and you haven't spoken to them much since, it's not required (as a matter of etiquette). It doesn't make sense either, if it means cutting good friends of recent times. Friends drift apart—that's natural. So ask yourself this: would your old friend invite you to his wedding if it was being held now? You should also contrast wedding size when considering the payback invite. If your mate had 300 and you're having 80, then don't feel obligated.

Yours, Hers and Ours

Ask whether a person is just *your* friend or your bride's friend or is truly friends with both of you. You'll both have very good friends at the wedding the other doesn't know well. However, when you're getting to the margins, going with 'our friends' over *yours* or *hers* can be a helpful culling factor.

Who Knows Who

If you have an odd man out—someone who will know no one else at the wedding—that can be a reason to cull as well. There was only one law school friend I was still in touch with so I cut him in the end, partly because I didn't think he'd have much fun at the wedding.

SAY 'NO' TO A NO LIST

One groom's advice book suggests creating a list of people you do *not* want at the wedding. This is a great idea if you want to spend the next week in a tearful screaming match with your bride. You're certain not to like some of your bride's friends or family, and the same will go for her (especially your mate who threw up in her wardrobe last New Year's Eve). Still, setting that down in a list is asking for big trouble. You might as well load up some pistols, line up back-to-back and start marching ten paces.

Instead, take such people on an individual basis and make reasonable compromises. If you don't like someone that is very important to your partner then let it slide, and she should do the same. On the other hand, if there is someone on your 'non-essential' list that your partner can't stand—especially if she has good reason—then let that person go. One of my non-core friends missed out because he never made any effort to talk to my partner on repeated occasions, and fair enough.

PEOPLE CAN BE WEIRD ABOUT THEIR KIDS

You may have an informal reception in mind, like an outdoor barbecue, with kids running around flying kites, chasing butterflies or whatever they do. Alternatively, you may be planning a formal evening reception that begins after bedtime for your average crayon-chucker, and you don't want grumpy kids crying, interrupting toasts or knocking over the ice sculptures. It's absolutely, 100 per cent your call. Why do I emphasise? Because *people can be weird about their kids.*

When people have kids, they naturally become the centre of their universe, which deludes some parents into believing they are the centre of everyone else's universe. That you would not want little Lucy or Rudiger at your wedding is inconceivable to them. This is just one of those times when you have to unapologetically play the 'it's my wedding' card, because children fundamentally change the nature of your reception and no one should force that on you or guilt you into it (especially for what kids' meals cost).

You Must be 'This High' to Attend Our Wedding

There are, however, some common compromises you can make with children:

1. *Age limit.* In our case, the children who would have come to the wedding were all under ten and most were under six. At that age, children are unable to appreciate a wedding and will probably be hugely

bored. They can also be disruptive during the ceremony and the reception. By ten or so, most kids are capable of sitting still and better able to appreciate what's going on (even if they're delightfully confused by some of the toasts). So, some couples invite children only above a certain age.

On the other end of the spectrum are newborns who, for practical reasons, can't be without their mother for long. It's reasonable to make an exception for them. Fortunately, newborns sleep most of the time and can be whisked away if they make too much of a racket.

2. *Split invite.* You can invite children to the ceremony, but not the reception. That way they're involved in the day, but don't intrude on the more adult festivities. You may have to deal with a bit of stirring, outbursts and crying during your vows, but responsible parents should take uppity children outside.

3. *Money's no object.* Some couples have a separate area at the reception for children, with games, activities, carers and even entertainers (clown, magician, etc.). That's terrific, but hard to swing if you don't have unlimited resources. Parents *should not* expect you to go to these lengths, but it's considerate to scout out babysitting options for parents travelling to your wedding with children, especially if you're inviting kids to the ceremony but not the reception.

Of course, some parents are happy to be kidless for the night (even if they bitched when their kids weren't invited).

WE LIKE KIDS

I sound like I don't like kids, but it's quite the opposite. My wife and I enjoy taking our nieces and nephews to the zoo, the beach and museums. Invariably, there are difficulties, tantrums, meltdowns, etc. and that's fine, because that's what kids do. But there's a time and place for baby vomit and toddler tantrums, and that's the Royal Easter Show, not a $100 per plate wedding reception.

Freed from baby talk, chastising and chasing, they get to be the fun-loving scamps you knew before children sucked out their energy. Selfishly, we wanted the parents we knew to be people again for this one evening. We wanted to enjoy their company without hearing, 'Timmy, don't smash your sister's inhaler—she needs that to live!'

ULTIMATUM VS PARENTAL DUTIES

You may have relatives or friends who, out of righteous indignation, threaten not to come to your wedding if their children are not welcome (yes, this actually happens). If they have so completely lost perspective that they think their children are of overriding importance on *your* wedding day, then they are beyond help, hope or prayers. Let them stay home and watch *The Wiggles Go Wigglin'* for the fortieth time. However, it's completely different if the parents *want* to come but can't, because they have newborns, sick children or otherwise can't arrange a sitter. If your friends can't make it work, you need to respect that their parental duties come first.

An Unfoolish Consistency with the Hobgoblins

Whatever rules you make as far as kids go (age restriction, reading test, height requirement) *you must be consistent.* Parents may get cranky when their kids aren't invited, but they should understand a 'no kids under twelve' policy and get over it. However, if their ten-year-old is left out and another ten-year-old is included, there will be hell to pay.

Uninviting the Little Ones

A children-friendly invitation should say 'Mr and Mrs Smith, Bonnie Smith, Clyde Smith' or 'Mr and Mrs Smith and family'. If it doesn't mention 'family' or the children specifically it's *supposed* to mean children are not invited, though not everyone is fully versed on the intricacies of wedding invitation etiquette. Hopefully, guests who are unsure will ask and not assume that children are invited, but don't count on it. For reasons passing understanding, etiquette prohibits useful information on your invitation such as 'adults only'. So be sure to actively spread the word through your parents, the guest grapevine, your wedding website, pony express and other wedding communiqué, as these painfully indirect methods are happily authorised by the mavens of etiquette.

OTHER HANGERS ON

What if you really want your good friend Dave at your wedding but you would rather not see his shrill, obnoxious shrew of a girlfriend, who treats him like crap? Where you draw the line with partners, as with other guest list rules, requires consistency.

As a start, you really have to invite wives/husbands, fiancés/fiancées and cohabitating partners, even if you don't know them (or like them). It's rude and a bit ridiculous not to. After that, it's your call. You may want to invite a friend's partner if it's reasonably serious, even if they haven't officially moved in yet. In a couple of cases, we even let a friend know verbally that their partner was welcome where the relationship had meaningfully progressed after we sent the invitations out.

Strangers in the Night

I would draw the line at the 'date' or 'plus one' invite, for a number of reasons.

1. You have a limited budget and limited space, so why would you want any of your guest list taken up by people you are unlikely to know well, if at all?
2. It can put pressure on a guest to 'find a date' for your wedding.
3. Most importantly, weddings are the ultimate hook-up venue. When I was a single lad, I would never bring a date to a wedding. You're surrounded by single women who are captivated by the romance of the event, the alcohol and the dancing, and who are damn jealous of the bride (jealousy being the ultimate aphrodisiac). The bridesmaids tend to be particularly amorous. (There's an old saying about bridesmaids—I think it's Voltaire—that goes: 'The uglier the dress, the quicker it comes off.') Hook-up stories are one of the best parts of any wedding, and

it's not unusual for people who share a sweaty night at a wedding to end up sharing their own wedding down the track.

THE MEAT MARKET GAME

A fun, wholesome wedding game to play with your bride:

1. Note all the single people attending your wedding.
2. Separately come up with a list of five potential hook-ups, assigning 50 points for your most likely pairing down to 10 points for the least likely.
3. Now, the fun part. You and your bride do whatever you like to make your competing matches happen, short of telling them about the game, spiking drinks or anything else that might get you arrested.
4. If your 50-point match hooks up you get 50 points, and so on down your match list (40, 30, 20 and 10 points). It's good strategy if both halves of your 50-point couple have demonstrated a certain 'moral flexibility' in the past.
5. As you gather the post-wedding hook-up stories, you each add up points to see who wins (stakes to be determined by you and your bride beforehand).

Sadly, we didn't get to play 'Meat Market' at our wedding—too many of our friends had already found happiness in someone else. It was very disappointing.

COMMON GUEST LIST ISSUES

The following are prickly guest list issues that often arise, and some general guidance.

You're an Orphan, She's Italian

If your partner has a much bigger family than you (or vice versa) it isn't reasonable to insist on a 50/50 guest split. You and your family should give a little, but you shouldn't miss out on close relatives or friends coming for the sake of all 47 of her cousins.

Money Talks

Does it matter who's paying? There are varying opinions, but hell yes, it does. It's your wedding, but if her parents (and/or yours) are footing the bill then it's only fair to include friends of the family, parental work colleagues, etc. who aren't at the top of your personal invite list. But they shouldn't overwhelm your wedding. If they do, and the parents won't cut back, you may have to face a more modest wedding on your own dime (or at least threaten it, to get your way).

If you're paying, then it's your show. Parents should have input, particularly on family, and you should be sensitive to requests, but don't get stuck paying for dozens of parental friends and work colleagues that you'd rather weren't there. Even if the 'rents are willing to pay the extra cost, you still have the right to say 'No'. Just be tactful. Shouting 'Well, I'm paying for the damn thing' is a nasty thing to say, especially if your parents or hers don't have the resources to contribute.

The Phantom Invite

Inviting people who you *know* can't make it can be tricky. There's a waning rule of etiquette saying that an invitation obligates a gift, regardless of attendance. So, it could look like you're fishing for gifts. Frankly, I find this rule a bit strange. I would not expect a gift from someone who couldn't make it to the wedding, though we got some, nonetheless. It tends to be generational, with gifts from non-attendees coming from aunts, uncles or older family friends but not from the gen X and Y slackers.

On the flip side, you could insult people close to you by not inviting them, even if they can't attend. I would err on the side of inviting rather than not, especially if they're close family or friends. You can let the word slip that gifts are not expected from people who can't attend. You'll still get some, but only because those invitees *want* to get you something, not because they feel obligated by a dubious etiquette requirement.

Casual Invites

No one should casually invite people to your wedding, including you. While Ricko from the cricket team is a great guy to do shots with, your partner may have other ideas. Before you nail down the budget and guest numbers, you can't make any promises outside of close friends and family. To dissuade other casual inviters (your parents, her parents or some other culprit), put them on the financial hook for any guests they add before the list is finalised.

Get Ahead on the 'Rents

Don't assume that your parents *won't* assume things. They may have the weddings of their day in mind, when it was more common for friends and colleagues of the parents to attend the wedding. Don't let *their* expectations get ahead of *your* planning. If they start casually inviting folks, it could lead to hardship for you or embarrassment for them.

Work Colleagues

This is a tricky wicket. If you don't invite everyone in your team, you risk offending people and damaging your working relationship. It's like when you were seven and had to invite all the kids in your class to your birthday party, including Wendell Weiner, who smelt like wet cabbage. Except now, Wendell makes the desk assignments and you don't want to end up in the storage closet. Still, inviting your whole team could put significant pressure on your budget.

It's certainly fair to invite the people that you have true friendships with outside the office (i.e., you regularly spend time with them outside of work and work functions). My partner invited only one person from her office, who was an old friend from back home. Anything beyond that risks exploding your guest list or creating tensions in the workplace.

Split Invitation

Some books recommend the split invitation cop-out: invite some people to the ceremony, but not the reception. It can work for kids, but otherwise it's a real kick in the guts: 'Thank you for witnessing a long-winded religious ceremony on rough-hewn pews. We're going to go get drunk, dance and laugh now, but we'd like you to go home.' Couples who use split invites should get a nice, big shiny box with no gift inside.

6

THE BUDGET

And You Thought Lehman Brothers Was Bad

'By far the biggest source of stress and shock in
wedding planning is realizing how much this day is
going to set you back. This is particularly difficult
for most grooms to comprehend'
(Weatherly 2005, p. 23).

. . . For once they speaketh the truth.

Wedding budgets are like the financial statements of large, complex and heavily leveraged investment banks. The budgetary figure obscures certain 'exploding costs', 'off-balance sheet transactions' and 'toxic debt' that don't materialise until far too late—except it's backed by *your* mortgage. Expenses can easily double your planned budget if you don't watch it like a forensic accountant on Ritalin. You could always entrench your wedding so deeply in the national economy that it simply becomes 'too big to fail' and the government will be forced to bail out your nuptials. But that could never happen in a modern, free-market economy, eh, comrade?

There's no shortage of advice on how to set and stick to a wedding budget—what's lacking is the *will*. Every time there's a decision between *more* and *less*, you'll hear from parents, friends, busybodies, and definitely from wedding professionals, 'but this is the most important day in your life' (i.e., $$$$$). But it's not the *only* day in your life. You have your honeymoon, for starters. Are you saving to buy a house? Do you need a new car? Are you relocating? Are you having children soon? All these things require money and planning. Even if the parents are paying, I'm sure you want to leave them something for their retirement.

So, when confronted with yet another expense, stop, take a deep breath (both of you) and think about all the things more important to you than silver-gilded wedding programs. Remember, no family member worth your time, and no friend worth having, is going to think less of you for not spending beyond your means on your wedding.

NEITHER A BORROWER NOR A PROCRASTINATOR BE

There are couples who go into debt to have 'the perfect wedding' (which is a furphy). Other couples wait to get married until they can afford the wedding they ought to have. Do neither. If you're in love and ready to be married, then get married. The flowers, ribbons, fancy food, limos and the lot are all trappings—mere wrapping paper. Don't leverage your future for their sake. All you need for a great wedding is your friends and family to celebrate with you, and you can do that at your community church, a backyard or a barbecue in a public park and you'll still be just as married.

DETERMINING THE BUDGET

Your first bit of budget planning is to decide what you can afford. Don't just think about the money you have but about what other expenses you have coming as well. Here are a few examples:

1. *Honeymoon.* You may not know what you're doing for your honeymoon or the exact cost, but get a general idea (consider flights, accommodation, travel insurance, etc.). The groom often takes the lead on the honeymoon, so make sure you leave some funds aside for the ultimate after party.
2. *Home.* If you already own a home, then you have a mortgage to pay. If you want to buy a home, then you

need savings for a deposit, stamp duty, transaction costs, etc. Don't blow your chance at a home for the sake of one party.

3. *Children.* We all love the little scamps, but the smaller they are the more stuff they need. You'll want a little in reserve when they come along.

4. *Life.* Do you need a new car? Are you relocating in the near future? Do your parents need help with medical bills? Think about all the things you want in your lives together, all your obligations, what they'll cost and how you'll save for them.

A wedding is a major expense. People tend to budget for weddings in an alternate reality bubble, isolated from all other monetary considerations. Instead, you need to consider it together with all of your other major life expenses. In short, *don't mortgage your marriage to pay for your wedding.*

BUDGET CONFERENCE

Your bride will probably lead the budget-busting charge (spurred by money-grubbing wedding professionals), simply because she cares more about wedding stuff than you. I'm sure you tend to go over budget on other things (the 50-inch plasma is only a grand more than the 40-inch—you'd be stupid *not* to buy it).

Honey, I Love You—Now Put Down the Credit Card and Back Away Slowly

There are hundreds of purchasing decisions throughout the wedding process. For each one there is a temptation to go that one level higher (as they said in the seminal mocku-mentary *This is Spinal Tap*, 'this one goes to 11'), stretching the budget that little bit more. But stressing restraint to your bride makes you a cheap, uncaring bastard. So, to counter the spending impulse, don't talk about money itself but about all the other things you want for the two of you (noted above). Putting your budgetary concerns this way shows that you *do* care but that you're thinking about your marriage, not just your wedding.

Also, beware of the 'one-up factor': 'Friends rush to outdo friends, competing over the number of attendants, the type of decorations, the menus—every detail of these elaborate productions' (Shervan and Sniechowski 2005, p. 48). You might hear, 'Well, Darlene had an ice sculpture at her wedding.' Respond with something sensitive, like, 'Well, when the thing melted, Darlene was still married to a complete twit.' Having a better husband outweighs the better wedding, over time.

DOWN WITH DOWRIES AND PANTALOONS

Tradition has it that the bride's family pays for most of the wedding. I know that we grooms and our kin have lived large off this for centuries, but it just doesn't make sense any more (remember, you could have daughters one day). It isn't even the norm. In both the US and Australia, the bride's parents pay for the whole wedding less than 30 per cent of the time.

The economy no longer depends on women coming to a marriage with 100 head of sheep and 350 acres of prime bottomland. Moreover, nothing guarantees that the bride's parents have more means than the groom's parents (I'd wager it only happens about half the time). Despite this, we still get the following from the mavens of etiquette: 'Manners still lead the way. It is still not correct for the bride's family to ask the groom's family to pay any of the wedding costs. If, however, his family offers to pay a share, it is quite appropriate for the bride's parents to accept' (Post 2006, p. 38). Post has the parents circling around each other in some kind of English Morris dance.

Let's eliminate these theatrics and the defunct presumption that the bride's parents pay, which should have gone out with pantaloons. It's not like people get married in their mid-teens these days (outside of *Home and Away*)—brides and grooms usually have their own resources. So, you and your partner should take the lead by considering your own finances and then approaching your respective parents about what they can contribute. Of course, if you and your partner are young and just starting out in life, then you'll need to depend more on your parents. Whatever their contribution is, however, it should be accepted with gratitude, not taken as an entitlement, and THAT is good manners.

This allows logic to sort out the relative contribution of the families, with factors like who has more money to give, who is asking for more guests and the like. In this world we all have different means and it's hardly the measure of any of us, so let's put pride and bad feelings aside.

REJECT EXTORTION

Funding from parents does not give them licence to dictate everything about your wedding. However, as in politics, it does give them a voice. Try to compromise, not just because they're footing the bill, but because they're your parents and future parents-in-law. Still, neither has the right to force you into a religious service, if that goes against your beliefs; nor should they make the wedding into something you never wanted. If they threaten to pull their funds, stand tall and threaten to go it on your own, even if that means a more modest wedding.

YOUR FAMILY'S CONTRIBUTION

Because of lingering traditions, and pride, your family's generosity could be taken as an insult. So tact is very important. If your family wants to make a significant contribution to the wedding, it's probably better for them to talk it over with you first rather than approaching your bride's family directly. That gives you the chance to talk it over with your partner, gauge how her parents might react and determine the best way of approaching them.

You can tell her parents that you believe the tradition of the bride's family paying for most things is outdated, unfair and no longer typical (use my well-reasoned arguments or, better yet, buy them a copy of my book). Still, your family should be wary of offering to pay more than half the costs, especially if they have greater means than your bride's family. Likewise, you and your family should be careful about making demands for a grander wedding than her parents can afford. In the end, the relationship between the families is more important than the extravagance of the wedding.

Of course, your parents may be counting on the bride's family to pay. I know it's hard to put upon your parents, but you may want to note the changing traditions, using the arguments above (or, even better yet, make a gift of this book). If your parents still have their heels dug in tradition, then either you and your bride can kick in more or you can lower your ambitions for the wedding.

CAN'T VS WON'T

If your bride's family can't pay, even etiquette says it's okay to go to your family for assistance, but do so in a way that won't hurt her parents' pride even if it means having a more modest wedding. If the bride's family *won't* pay, because they disapprove, and your parents are happy to front up, then go nuts. No need to spare feelings any more—they're the ones who've insulted you.

WHAT WORKS FOR YOU

Most importantly, the division of costs and responsibilities should work for you and your circumstances. My wife and I are from two different countries, across the world from each other. We were happy to pay for and organise our wedding in Sydney, where we lived. Her parents made a generous contribution, which we gratefully accepted.

In the US it's traditional for the groom's family to host a 'rehearsal dinner' (so named because it follows the ceremony rehearsal) for the bride and groom's immediate family and the wedding party. My parents offered to do that for us in Sydney. However, rehearsal dinners aren't as common in Australia. And we knew that many of my friends and family wouldn't be able to make it from the States for the Sydney wedding. More important to us was having a party to celebrate our wedding with them the next time we were back in New York. It would have been hard for us to organise the New York party from Australia, and hard for my US-based parents to organise a rehearsal dinner in Sydney.

So we asked my parents if they could throw the party in New York, and instead of a rehearsal dinner in Sydney we organised an informal barbecue as a relaxed way for the families to get to know each other. It all worked out very well, because we didn't bind ourselves with tradition and we did what made the most sense for us in our circumstances, and if you do that you can't go wrong (well, you can, but you're less likely to).

Fundraising Limits

You or your bride may have a well-off aunt, uncle or godparent who is willing to help with expenses. It's best to let them approach you, unless you decide to have wedding sponsors (see '*Padrinos* and *Madrinas*' box on p. 102). You don't want to appear grabby and you want to avoid any insult to your bride's parents or yours. You could have these generous rellies pay for a particular part of the wedding (the bar, the band, etc.) and have that be their wedding present. Alternatively, they could give you a cash wedding gift. As money is fungible (a dollar here is the same as a dollar there), you can use it to help with your wedding expenses.

PADRINOS AND *MADRINAS*

Latin American weddings feature *padrinos* and *madrinas*, who are usually close friends of the family (like godparents). They act as spiritual guides and mentors to the couple, and also sponsor some part of the wedding (wedding bands, dress, grog, etc.). There can be multiple *padrinos* and *madrinas* sponsoring different aspects of the wedding. It's considered an honour and it's a way of involving more intimately in the wedding the people who have been important to you or your bride.

Sponsoring doesn't have to mean money. A keen gardener can provide flowers, a baker friend can do the cake and a mate might drive you to the wedding in his classic car. So, if you don't need more things for your kitchen, then think of asking some of your nearest and dearest to be sponsors as an *alternative* to giving you a gift you don't need. It's not an English-speaking tradition, but if you don't ask for too large a contribution (more than a nice wedding gift), you explain that you want to involve them in the wedding to honour them, and you acknowledge their role in the wedding program and toasts, then I think most people will be chuffed. If not, say 'never mind' and they can get you that monogrammed toaster you never wanted.

COST CUTTING

You have to plan your budget before you start locking things in. If you overspend on a major item before factoring in everything else, you'll either short-change other elements of your wedding or end up way over budget. Here are a few ways to stay in the black.

Time to Excel

There are so many little details that go into a wedding, you can't hope to keep track of them in your head. Use spreadsheet or budgeting software to detail all your planned expenditures. This makes it much easier to monitor your expenses and make adjustments along the way.

You can make your own spreadsheet from scratch, start with a friend's or download a template from the internet (search for 'wedding budget template'). The main wedding websites now have budget planners built into their sites, rather than providing downloadable templates (to keep you going back and seeing the ads). They might work for you, but will be less flexible.

Down Over/Under

In your budget spreadsheet, have one column for your estimate of an item's cost and the next column for the actual cost (once that's determined). Then, include an 'over/under' column that subtracts the actual cost from the estimate. That will tell you how much you're off budget for that item. At the bottom of the over/under column, have a total that's continually updated. This gives you a running tally of how much you're going over your set budget. You'll see quickly how a lot of little deviances can add up to a budget blowout. See the Appendix on p. 289 for a sample budget.

Unknown Unknowns

There *will* be expenses that you don't plan for (what former US defence secretary Donald Rumsfeld called 'unknown unknowns') or that you underestimate. You can anticipate them by putting a reserve into your budget of around 10 to 20 per cent (i.e., if you have $10,000 to spend, leave a reserve item of about $1500 in your initial budget). This can be tapped as your *unknowns* make themselves known. The reserve may seem large, but considering that couples regularly double their planned spend it might not be nearly enough. Of course, the contingency must *stay* a contingency. If you rely on your reserve every time you're faced with a potential cost that's over your budget, you'll blow through it very quickly. Leave the reserve for unexpected costs, not for going over budget on every item.

Cut the Pointless Crap

There's so much crap that people try to sell you and your bride in connection with a wedding. Remember that you're *on a budget* and resist the urge to buy monogrammed toasting glasses, aisle runners, a live butterfly release, decorated sugar cubes, and all other similar junk. You don't need it. Don't buy it.

Spare a Thought for Cousin Eddie

If your expenses start to blow out, you may have to cut the guest list to stay on (or near) your budget. So, when you're debating those engraved wedding menus, spare a thought for cousin Eddie with the lazy eye and the lisp before he gets culled, because Eddie doesn't get out much.

Friday I'm in Love

Setting aside their new wave hairstyles, there's much in what The Cure says. You'll have greater availability and lower pricing if you avoid a Saturday wedding. Friday can work well, with a late afternoon ceremony and evening reception. A Sunday morning wedding with a brunch reception will also save you a bundle. Sunday evening is doable, but may be hard on people who have to travel or for working people (Monday hangovers suck). You can also save by marrying in less popular times of year. March and November are peak months for weddings in Australia, while the winter months are less in demand.

What Really Matters?

Figure out what's important to both of you and what isn't. We really wanted a friend of ours to play with his band at the wedding. This cost more than we budgeted for music but it was important to us, whereas we didn't need professional invitations (we did them ourselves), wedding programs (did without), or fancy wedding cars (no one was going to see them). We also managed to come in under budget on other items, like the photography, because of a good recommendation. As with any budget, it's okay if certain items come in a little over as long as that's offset by savings elsewhere (just keep track of your over/under column).

Tax Deductions (Kerry Packer–style)

You can write a book about weddings for men, then deduct your wedding expenses as 'research' (at least, that's what I'm taking to my accountant).

CASH BAR

Couples are absolutely prohibited from passing any wedding-related expenses along to guests. That means that you are absolutely forbidden to have a cash bar at your wedding. There are no exceptions to this rule, ever (Shaw 2001, p. 31).

Screw that. This advice from Kim Shaw is a consistent decree in the wedding books, and it's a crock. Wedding planners are used to dealing with brides who got doll-houses when they were nine that cost more than the real houses I can't afford now, but in the real world weddings cost money. Money is rent. Money is mortgage payments. Money is petrol. Money is health care.

Two friends of mine got married years back and they didn't have any help from their parents, or much money of their own, so they had a cash bar. Anyone who goes to a wedding should assume the couple is providing as much as they can with the resources they have. We all understood and appreciated the food, music and everything else. We were happy to pay for our drinks. I know this sounds a little old-fashioned, but we also thought the point of the occasion was to celebrate their wedding, not to tick off wedding features.

If budgetary constraints force you to go with a cash bar or make any other concessions to financial constraints, then you may very well offend the Kim Shaws of the world. On the bright side, at least you won't have to listen to them drone on any more about how ungrateful and lazy today's servants are.

7

THE PROFESSIONALS

Your 'Wedding Team'

*'The caterer is an important member
of your wedding team'*
(Post 2006, p. 269).

. . . That's funny, because when the guys with
exposed bum-cracks moved my stuff, I never
considered them part of my 'moving team'.

If you flip through the wedding books piling up on your coffee table (during a break in the footy match), you'll see that they're written by wedding planners and other industry insiders who talk up other members of their industry as part of your 'wedding team'. Just like your movers, the people you hire for your wedding are being paid to do a service, do it professionally and hopefully not break stuff. They're not your friends, family or part of your 'team'. Of course, it's best to treat them with courtesy and respect. You get better service that way and, besides, it's what your mum taught you. In turn, it's crucial that you work with pleasant people. If you found a venue you like but the people there are dismissive, condescending or rude, then think twice. You don't want to deal with the stress and you *especially* don't want your bride dealing with it, because her stress will come back to you like a Wile E Coyote ACME deathtrap.

PRETTY (EXPENSIVE) LANGUAGE

'Wedding team' is just one of the pretentious and expensive words and phrases you'll encounter during the wedding process. You don't have an idea about your wedding, you have a '*vision*'; you're not having food but a '*culinary experience*'; and you're not paying for your wedding, you're having a '*financial enema*'. Other pricey words to look out for include: 'little touches' (or 'finishing touches'), 'flair', 'accoutrements', 'calligraphic', 'tailored', 'theme', 'elegant', 'luxury' and 'traditional'. They all translate to the same words for you: money, money and money.

WEDDING CONTRACTS

Wedding guides tell you to have written contracts for *everything* and to read them all carefully. Good advice, but in real life you'll probably be too busy. Even my contracts professor in law school admitted that he doesn't read half the stuff he signs. So, if you have limited time, be relaxed about the smaller things (printing of invitations) and focus on the big things (caterer and reception venue). Make sure everything is clear to you and that key items like dates, timing and delivery are specified. Also look for the following:

1. *Cancellation.* Check the clauses on cancellations, refunds, postponements or making any other changes and any related drop-dead dates (e.g., if you cancel after a certain date, you lose your deposit or owe the entire amount).

2. *Tips and taxes.* Check whether gratuities, service charges and taxes are included in the quoted price and, if not, what they'll be (or are expected to be). People you might tip include: waiters and bartenders, parking attendants, coat check, bathroom attendants (but they're creepy—do without) and limo/car drivers. Sort out tips ahead of time, where possible. Otherwise have tips ready in envelopes on the day.

3. *Timing of payments.* If you're on a tight personal budget, take note of the *timing* of payments as well. You'll have some upfront deposits but also note when *full* payments are due, which can be weeks ahead of the wedding day.

4. *Flat rate or cut.* If you're hiring a wedding planner, does she charge a flat rate, an hourly rate or a percentage of the budget? The percentage approach creates very bad incentives: the more your wedding costs, the more she gets paid. Just to give you a sense of how bad an idea this is, it's how the US government pays its defence contractors, who invariably go billions over budget.

5. *Per head or per bottle.* If you go per bottle, make sure you trust your caterer. Again, it creates bad incentives (clearing half-full glasses, opening new bottles with unfinished bottles still sitting on tables, overestimating consumption, etc.). So, make sure you have a firm understanding with the caterer on how the alcohol will be served. On the flip side, if you go per head, make sure they're not too stingy with the grog.

TOO PRECIOUS

'Don't be guilty of showing one caterer's proposal to another caterer . . . you'll instantly be elevated to uber-Bridezilla status' (Weatherly 2005, p. 59). Screw that. What do you care? The wedding professionals who write books are a bit precious about other wedding professionals. First off, don't tell the other caterer that you shared some of their ideas. Second, how many weddings do you plan on having? Do you really care about your reputation in the industry? This is hopefully a one-off for you two.

Do You Have a Nice Package?

One major decision is whether you eat where you sit, so to speak, meaning that your food is provided by your reception venue, as with restaurants and most hotels. It makes planning easier if everything comes together. You're dealing with fewer vendors, fewer contracts and one inclusive price (potentially, at a discount). It will be a large price, but it will constitute the lion's share of your reception expenses. Hotels can offer particularly good package deals, with discounted rooms, free parking, use of hotel vans for transport, etc. On the other hand, these package deals can limit your flexibility and you have to be happy with the space, food, rooms and everything else. All things considered I favour simplicity, but what groom wouldn't?

Still, be aware of the 'complete wedding package' rort from all types of wedding vendors, which is the privilege of paying more for nearly nothing in return. When investigating venues, go Magnum PI and suss out what a similarly sized corporate event or birthday party would cost at the same venue (a quick phone call or check of the website). If their 'wedding package' is significantly more, find out *exactly* what that extra money gets you. It isn't always a rip-off. The additional cost may reflect things you want at a reasonable price (e.g., a dance floor, wedding cake, tables, chairs, linens). However, it could just mean that you're having a *wedding* and they think they can gut you.

If that's the case, negotiate the price down or drop them like a steaming cow pat and choose another venue or vendor. Whether it's a rort or not, try to knock off parts of the package you don't want (e.g., decorations, valet parking, a

> ### DON'T CHEAT THE CHEATERS
>
> *Do not* pretend you're having some other type of event and then show up for a wedding reception. It's too clever by half—the venue will cotton on at some point. You run the risk that they'll pull the plug or add extra costs, because you didn't read clause 27(g)(ix) of your contract. Most importantly, the last thing you want on your wedding day is to go four rounds with the venue managers or caterers.

TRUST ME

Why trust me? You've already bought my book, so I'm covered. I don't make more money because you decide to pay for valet parking at your reception and I don't have any friends who do either.

soup course) for a corresponding reduction in price. They want your business and should be flexible, within reason. You can also try to get some other extras thrown in the package instead, for no cost or at a discount. It might be easier than negotiating on price.

DON'T BE AVERAGE, BE YOU

Always consider the source when it comes to how much you *should* spend on your wedding or any part of it. If you're talking to wedding professionals, planners or anyone who gets a cut, of course they are going to talk up the cost (what you 'simply *must* have'). Most 'average' figures in wedding books, magazines and the internet come from the wedding industry, which has a vested interest in inflating them.

Bride to Be magazine's most recent online 'Cost of Love' survey put forth an astronomical sum for an 'average' Australian wedding, which was repeatedly quoted by the mainstream media. These magazine and industry surveys are not Gallup, Newspoll or Nielsen and are not scientific. At best, the *Bride to Be* figure reflects the cost of the average wedding among *Bride to Be* readers. These brides may be much wealthier, or have wealthier families, than the typical bride and are certainly more interested in wedding extravagance. In polling language, *Bride to Be* didn't have a representative sample (a cross-section of couples from different socio-economic backgrounds in proportions reflecting such variations in Australian society).

When the wedding industry throws out these outlandish figures the media quotes the number because it makes a good story ('look how crazy people get with their wedding, now back to the genocide in Darfur'). That spurs you and your families to spend more on your wedding, to keep up with illusory friends and neighbours. Fortunately, I'm not mired in the wedding industry cabal, so I'm not going to tell you the *average* cost of an Australian wedding. First, I don't know. Second, I don't trust the figures I've seen. Third, it doesn't matter. The 'average' cost of a wedding is a furphy. Weddings vary wildly in type, style and cost. You have to have the wedding that's right for you and bugger everyone else.

Friends

When setting your budget, you need some idea of what needs to go in and what things will cost. Wedding books and websites provide exhaustive budget templates that list all the potential items. Just include what applies to you. As for costs, the best approach is to talk to friends, family and work colleagues who've had weddings in recent years.

Some may be uncomfortable talking about money (or will be embarrassed about what they spent), but you don't have to talk specifics. Based on the research they did for their wedding, they can give you a general sense of what things cost. They may have their own spreadsheets to give you (we passed on our budget template to two other couples). You can trust your friends to give you good and helpful information, and you can also learn from the mistakes they made so you can avoid the same pitfalls.

AND THE BAND PLAYED ON

'Your band or DJ is one of the key elements of your reception, to treat them with anything less than the utmost deference and respect is a breach of good manners' (Shaw 2001, p. 191). Suddenly wedding bands are divas and you have to pick out all the yellow M&M's from their dressing-room stash—this is what happens when you believe the wedding books.

Last Night an iPod Saved My Life

Not that I want to put all cheesy DJs out of business (well, I kinda do), but the MP3 revolution makes them pretty unnecessary. (Really, we're talking about iPods. I don't mean to insult anyone who has a non-iPod MP3 player; I'm sure it was really cool to have a Betamax VCR too, and who can forget the eight-track player.) An iPod lets *you* choose the songs you want played at your reception and without the expense of a DJ or band. You can make separate lists for the cocktail hour and during the meal (softer background music) then a dance mix for later, and save the raucous stuff for the after-party selection. If you don't have a song you want, just download it for loose change. Organising the music is a great way for a groom to contribute, though you'll probably have to throw your bride a few bones (I had to include three Kylie songs—shudder).

At the reception, just plug your iPod into the venue's speaker system or hire some sound equipment, if necessary. You'll want to nominate a groomsman to be a pseudo-DJ (start and stop the right mix at the right time) because you *do not* want to deal with active DJ duty on the day. I've been the iPod DJ for several friends' weddings.

A word of caution: DJ or not, people will still make requests. Once you set the dance mix playing, tell everyone the iPod is encased in an adamantium time-lock vault which will only open when the reception ends or at the Rapture, whichever comes first. And in case there are any problems with the iPod, make sure you have a backup device with the playlists you want, or you can burn CDs with your mix.

Live Band

A live band is always a nice touch. If you find a band you like, they play enough songs you want and you can afford it, then go nuts. Your own experience at weddings and word of mouth are crucial when selecting a band, because many are painfully bad. (The audition scene from 1998's *The Wedding Singer*, with Adam Sandler and Drew Barrymore, provides an instructive example.) Your reception venue managers or wedding planner may have recommendations, though friends will know your tastes better. A friend of ours is a terrific musician and he put together a great band for us, featuring himself.

With this option you lose some flexibility in the range of music for your wedding, as even the most flexible bands have limitations, but you can always have a band play background music for cocktails and the meal and some old standards for the early dancing then hit the iPod later for some gen X tunes, which is what we did. If you have a band, one or more of them might also provide the music for your ceremony. Our friend (the violinist from the band) played music in the lead-up to the ceremony, as well as the processional and recessional.

General Principles

If you go with a band or DJ, they'll have a playlist. Beyond the official dances (your first dance, bride dancing with her dad, etc.), you'll probably want to pick a few more songs that you definitely want played during the evening. Even more importantly (especially with a DJ) you want a '*Do Not*' playlist. Some people are 'Chicken Dance', 'Electric Slide' and 'Macarena' people and some people are not (I'm definitely in the latter camp). Make sure you let the DJ or band know which camp you fall into. There should also be some general relation between the formality of your reception and your music. A grunge band at a black-tie affair is simply out of joint. Watch the particularly crude or violent songs too—you don't want Eminem pushing Grandpa Willie to an early grave, so save that for the after-party tune.

A PICTURE SAYS A THOUSAND DOLLARS

One way to ease some of the pressure off your bride is to take the lead on photography and video. It involves electronics, computers, chemicals and the like, so it's sufficiently male territory.

Photographer

Photography styles (like 'traditional', 'classical' and 'photojournalistic') are a bit like women. At the end of the day, you know what you like when you see it. Don't concern yourself too much with what these styles mean. Flip through the sample photos (portfolio) of the photographers you're considering. Go with the person who has the style, or mix of styles, that suits your taste best (or, more likely, your bride's). Black and white vs colour is also a matter of taste, though I would say it's nice to have a mix.

'1 FOR 2' SALE

'If your mother is steadfastly traditional and your idea of a great wedding portrait is you . . . standing in a field of wildflowers, you might want to think about hiring two photographers—traditional and artistic' (Shaw 2001, p. 211). Isn't it funny how the wedding book answer to a difference of opinion is to get both at twice the cost? Here's another idea. Find a photographer with some versatility in style or reach some other accommodation with your mother-in-law (unless she's paying, in which case get four photographers, if that helps).

Be Candid

To me, candid reception shots are the most fun and interesting. Your guests are being natural, milling about and talking to each other, so it captures the *vibe* of your wedding. Asking them to pose too much takes them out of the very moment you want to capture. If you want candids, make sure it's something your photographer does and does well (check his or her portfolio). Here's one of the favourite candids of two mates of mine from my own wedding:

If you really want to expand the universe of candid photos, you can leave disposable cameras on the tables for guests to use. Encourage them to focus on other guests (the photographer will take care of you two) and give them a central place to drop off the cameras. These days, however, many guests bring their digital cameras and get good quality wedding shots, so the disposables may be a bit redundant, but you can set up a common web page where everyone can upload their photos (e.g. www.flickr.com).

Balance is good, so it's nice to have some posed shots in the mix as well. Table shots (posed pictures of all the guests at each table) gets you at least one picture of every guest.

Timing

Most principal photography for the couple, the wedding party and close family occurs between the ceremony and the reception. Everyone's all frocked up and you're finally allowed to see your bride in her dress (assuming you've been adhering to tradition). Some couples do the shoot on some other day, though that seems a bit staged, not to mention a great inconvenience for everyone. Just don't let the post-ceremony shoot drag on forever by going through every possible combination of family and wedding party shot (male cousins born in even years, for instance). Otherwise, there's too much lag time for your guests or you miss too much of your own party. Trust me, when you've just been wed, the last thing you want to do is stand around forever having thousands of photos snapped. You'll get a burning desire to do a Harold Holt for the reception.

To minimise this painful interlude, you can do the photographs of the bride and her crew and you and your crew separately *before* the ceremony. Then you only have to do the joint photos post-ceremony. If neither you nor your bride are superstitious about her being seen in her dress pre-nuptials, then you can do the whole shebang before the ceremony. Whenever you do the photos, use your best man, groomsmen and ushers as photographer's assistants to help round up people for the shots and keep them from wandering off (as they tend to do).

Night and Day

It's easy to get out of hand with the photographs. Some brides want *everything* recorded, almost from the time she wakes up. This means pictures of her getting dressed with all her bridesmaids, getting their hair and make-up done, and so on. God help your photography budget if that's the way you go. If your bride really wants to capture these moments, friends with digital cameras can be counted on for some good shots, while saving the cost of the extra hours for the professional.

STILL LIFES

Some couples hire an additional photographer specialising in the 'commercial' style *just* to take pictures of the decor, flowers, cake, centrepieces, and so on. That seems a little excessive, as you'd think that any photographer who can shoot pictures of people should be able to manage stationary objects as well.

Focus on the Negatives

If at all possible, get your photographer to agree contractually to hand over the high-resolution digital files or negatives of your photos (low-resolution photos are not good enough for making quality prints). Your contract will likely include a certain number of prints prepared by your photographer. Ideally, you want to be able to run off additional copies for loose change at the local Kodak shop, as well as post photos on the internet, for friends and family. Many photographers will charge an arm and a leg for negatives or high-res digital files, and others won't even provide it as an option to ensure you get all your prints done through them. Try to find a photographer with a reasonable policy. We paid about $200 extra to get digital files of all our photos, which was a particularly good deal. If the photographer you want won't budge, at least have an upfront agreement on the cost of additional prints.

Video Guy

Like everything else with weddings videos are getting bigger and more complex, with a lot of additional production value, but as director Michael Bay has proven time and

(IN)FAMOUS WEDDING VIDEOS

The 'JK Wedding Entrance Dance' is the internet wedding video sensation of recent times. The featured wedding party does a *Glee*-type dance number down the aisle to the Chris Brown song 'Forever' (a dubious choice, given Brown's domestic violence conviction for his assault on fellow singer Rihanna). The video has had an astonishing 55 million views on YouTube and, in a nod to Brown's criminal actions, the couple now has a website (www.jkweddingdance.com) to encourage donations to a charity for the prevention of domestic violence. You just can't make up this stuff.

Another popular clip (with a modest 13 million YouTube views) is of a couple who start their first dance to 'Unchained Melody' only to have it interrupted by the hip-hoppery of Sir Mix-a-Lot's 'Baby Got Back' (a banned song in many wedding etiquette books). If you want to see a couple of goofy white folks dancing to rap, a YouTube search for 'wedding baby got back' will get you there. No word on whether the couple is encouraging donations to a charity for the prevention of violence against urban culture.

again with movies like *Transformers* and *Transformers 2*, bigger ain't always better. I was lukewarm on doing a video of our wedding, so we never got around to organising it. Eventually I asked a friend to record some of the ceremony on his camcorder. The video was short and simple and we were very glad to have it, especially for family who couldn't make it to the wedding. If you're not sure you want a video, you can't afford a video guy (the correct term is 'videographer' but I find that cumbersome and overly dramatic—and it sounds expensive) or you don't want the whole production, consider asking a friend to record *discrete* portions of your wedding, like your vows and first dance, but don't abuse his generosity by asking him to spend the whole day recording. If that's what you want, then hire someone.

General Principles

1. *Obtrusiveness.* Discuss with your photographer and video guy how 'in your face' they'll be. Some photographers have an uncanny talent for being constantly in the way. They're a huge distraction during the ceremony and pester everyone during the reception. You want good shots and good footage, but not at the cost of tainting your memories of the day and those of your guests.
2. *Don't get pushed around.* Don't let the photographer, video guy or anyone else control your day or bully you or your bride. They work for you. If you're missing the fun because the photographer wants a hundred shots that you don't care about, then call a stop to it or have your groomsmen run interference.

3. *Ceremony.* Check whether photography or video recording is prohibited or restricted in any way by your ceremony or reception venue. Some officiants may not allow photography at all or during certain parts of the ceremony and some reception venues may restrict the use of lighting equipment.

4. *Time.* One provision that should be clear in your contract is how long your photographer or video guy will be working on the day: how many hours total, what parts of the day they're covering (ceremony, reception, pre-game), arrival and departure times, etc.

5. *The list.* It's helpful to provide a list of the people and specific groups that you want captured in pictures and video. The photographer is likely to request a list of desired shots, and may have a suggested list for you to choose from (traditional wedding books also have such lists). Again, don't go over the top or you'll spend the whole day posing for photos, while making your wedding party and family do the same.

6. *Websites.* Photographers and video folks usually showcase their work on their websites. It's a great way to sample their wares and narrow down your choices, so you only have to meet with a few (or even one) before making your decision.

WHEELS

Church Bound and Down

You need to arrange transportation to and from the wedding for yourself and your bride; a big white dress and flowing

THE BANDIT

'East Bound and Down' is the irresistibly catchy theme song from *Smokey and the Bandit*. In the film, the Bandit (Burt Reynolds) picks up a runaway bride (Sally Field) in his black Trans Am during an interstate bootlegging run. The bride is running from the dimwitted son of Sherriff Buford T. Justice (Jackie Gleason), which is what happens when you don't get your bride a decent ride.

veil don't do well crammed into the crowded seating of a public bus. At least this chore involves cars, engines, motor oil and other manly things (though a pink limo with floral decorations may detract from the manliness—all the more reason for you to take charge). Feel free to enlist the help of the groomsmen. For example, one of them could drive you to the wedding.

Before forking out for the stretch Humvee limo, consider whether anyone will actually *see* you or your bride arrive or depart. A friend offered to drive my bride to our wedding in a restored 1936 Dennis fire engine, which would have been very cool except no one was going to see her arrive so it didn't seem worth the trouble.

Limo and sedan services often charge huge premiums for wedding transport for little value in return. Understand what that premium is and what you get for it, then decide whether you want the fancy ride or you just want to get from A to B.

Grooms Don't Let Guests Drink and Drive

If there's a significant distance between your ceremony, your reception and the hotel the blow-ins are staying at then consider providing transport for your guests, particularly if convenient public transport or affordable taxis aren't available. This is about public safety as much as convenience. Wedding receptions are like schoolies for adults, so you don't want your guests driving if it can be avoided. The hotel where your out-of-town guests are staying may have a van service you can use for free or at minimal cost. Otherwise, look into hiring a bus service (your hotel or reception venue may have recommendations). As a last resort, make taxi numbers available to your guests and contact the taxi services ahead of time to let them know that you'll need a number of taxis around the time your reception is ending.

OTHER STUFF

Here are a few bits and pieces that didn't fit neatly into the other sections.

Meals and Dress

If you have a band, photographer, or video guy hanging around for most of the reception it's expected that you provide them with food, so be sure to ask whether that's something they'll need (they might not). Your caterer should provide meals for these folks at a reduced price. The band may also require things like dressing space, so make sure your venue can accommodate them. Lastly, let all the professionals know the dress of your reception. Your photographer and band don't have to meet the dress standards for your guests, but you don't want the band sporting a Mötley Crüe look at your black-tie affair.

WEDDING INSURANCE

With the global financial crisis claiming mighty banks and small businesses alike, use of wedding insurance is on the rise. In case the wedding venue goes under, your bride gets a sniffle of the swine flu (no offence) or the region gets flooded, you may want some financial protection. Doing an online search for 'wedding insurance' will net you a few options. Unfortunately, the insurance doesn't cover 'cold feet' or a crap marriage, so make sure you've picked the right lass.

Amateur Hour

If you're looking to save money, consider hiring *future* professionals for your wedding. You can look to music schools for live music, art schools for photographers and film schools for video people. As they're not professionals, and working your wedding is part of their training, you can expect to pay much less for their services. Also, they haven't learned how to screw you yet. You're always taking a risk with people still learning their trade (I would draw the line at a P-plater for your limo driver), but if you're on a budget and particularly if it's a choice between an amateur or nothing, then it can't hurt to give them a go. And who knows, you may have the next Baz Luhrmann filming your wedding (let's just hope it turns out better than *Australia*).

Confirmation Saves Perspiration

Try to confirm as much as possible with your vendors at least two weeks before the wedding. That leaves time to fix any misunderstandings or make other arrangements if someone stuffs up. Fred and Wilma made the mistake of calling their water-taxi company just days before their wedding to discover that their reservation had vanished, and it would have been a long swim for the guests. These things happen, and all too often. Because they only found out last minute, they really had to scramble and it was added stress they didn't need. Do a

CLASSIC SEINFIELD

In a classic *Seinfeld* rant, Jerry responded to a rental car agent who had given away his car yet still insisted she knew why they have reservations: 'I don't think you do. If you did, I'd have a car. See, you know how to *take* the reservation. You just don't know how to *hold* the reservation. And that's really the most important part of the reservation—the *holding*. Anybody can just take 'em.'

call through of your vendors (catering, venue, transport, flowers, photographer, hotel, etc.) on a certain day about a fortnight out to confirm everything, including dates, times and important details. Even if your bride puts that list together, you can take a load off her shoulders by making some calls (you can even delegate a few to a friend or family member who's familiar with your plans, like a member of your wedding party). It will just take a couple of hours, but it will give you, and especially your bride, crucial peace of mind.

8

THE WHEN, THE
WHERE, THE HOW

*Here She Comes, Just a Walkin'
Down the Aisle*

'The[re] are few moments in life when we are
catapulted to a realm that defies our normal
conceptions of reality, time and space'
(Paul 2000, p. 141).

. . . It's a wedding, not *The Matrix*.

Much like a BASE-jumper, when you dive into a wedding it's very important to know where to jump off from. Some 'first things first' items are the date, the geographical location and *how* you will be married (whether in a religious or civil ceremony). These crucial preliminary matters are dealt with below, though before you get into any serious wedding planning you must also consider your *budget* (see Chapter 6). Happy diving!

DATE CERTAIN

When it comes to setting a date for the wedding, Turk, from the TV show *Scrubs*, speaks for many men:

> *Turk*: You know those lame-ass couples that get engaged, but they never actually get married—they just cruise along, year after year, without making any real kind of commitment?
>
> *JD*: Uh-huh.
>
> *Turk*: Dude, I wanted to be one of those couples, man!

The Burning Question

You will have one major motivation for setting a date. You'll get tired of answering the same damn question (in its many forms): 'So, when are you getting married/tying the knot/getting hitched/strapping on the ball and chain/taking the plunge . . .' and so on and so forth. Make no mistake, this question comes hard and fast. When you tell someone you're engaged, the next words out of their mouth are: 'So, have you set a date?' You can throw out random dates to mess with people, like 29 February (less funny if you're heading into a leap year), but that's a short-term fix. The question follows you like stink on a pig until you answer it. And the cold, hard truth of it is that if you weren't ready to set a date you probably weren't ready to propose.

All Things Wait for the Date

Setting your date will involve a combination of factors, such as the season, how long you want for planning, how much notice you need to give to family and friends to ensure they can be there, among others. Just remember that while three months may seem like plenty of time, for anything but the simplest weddings that's a rush job (crazy, but true). Popular wedding venues book up a year or more in advance and wedding gowns can take six months or more to tailor. So, don't be surprised if your partner is talking about anywhere from six to eighteen months. Of course, the necessary lead time varies depending on the size, scale and formality of the wedding. If you really want to get married in three months, or even three weeks, you can make it happen.

Once you have a general idea of your timing (and budget), you need to secure your ceremony and reception venues as they get booked out soonest. Additionally, most other planning revolves around your date and choice of venues, so there's no point doing much else until those are sorted. If you're looking to get married at the more popular times of year (November and March are the busiest months for weddings in Australia) the competition will be fiercer for top venues.

There's No Time Like Whenever

Know that there's no *perfect date* for your wedding. There's no date when every venue and vendor you want is available. There's no date when all your family and friends will be able to come. There's no date when the sun is guaranteed to shine. You try to get as much as you can, but you need to prioritise. If it's essential that you get married by the minister who's known you from childhood, then make that a requirement. If you want your friend's band to play at your wedding, then run your dates past him. You can even check the almanac to avoid the rainy seasons. Otherwise, there are plenty of celebrants, musicians, photographers and caterers in the sea, and your second or third choice of any of them will probably be pretty good.

Similarly, when dealing with a guest list of 100 or more people with different lives and schedules, not everyone will be able to come to *your* special day. But there are people that you or your bride could not imagine getting married without (e.g., your parents and your wedding party), so run your prospective dates by them. For the rest, all you can do is give as much notice as possible.

Holiday Weekends

If you're planning your wedding for a holiday weekend or during school holidays be sure to give *plenty* of notice, as people often make plans far ahead for those dates. Additionally, at many of those times your costs for venues and vendors may be higher and your guests' costs for hotels and airfares may be at a premium. It's best not to choose a weekend known for family trips or get-togethers. When my wife and I had a party in New York to celebrate with US friends and family who couldn't make it to our Sydney wedding, we chose the Fourth of July weekend. While it was great for my family, many of my friends couldn't make it because of their own family obligations.

Shotgun Wedding

Have you knocked up your best girl, and you want to do right by her? It doesn't just happen in the fifties, but some attitudes are stuck there: 'Brides may not move the wedding date until after the birth date "so I'll be able to drink and have a good time"' (Shaw 2001, p. 11). Why the hell not? It makes sense to me. One usually slender, pregnant bride offered another legitimate reason for postponement: 'I've never been anything more than a size 8, and I'm not going to start with my wedding dress.'

If the strain of planning a wedding on top of impending birth is too much to bear, then postpone the wedding. Alternatively, there's no law that says a wedding ceremony and celebration have to occur on the same day. You and your bride may want to be married before you have your baby, for reasons of religion, family or your own personal views (but not because some wedding book told you so). In that case, have a private wedding ceremony with close family and friends and have a larger celebration sometime after your child is born (a delayed reception). As a bonus, your wedding gifts can include baby stuff.

LOCATION, LOCATION, LOCATION

Will you get married where you and your partner live, where her family lives, where your family lives, or are all those one and the same? One important factor is how much you and your partner want to plan your own wedding. If you're having the wedding where the bride's family lives and that's across the country from you, then simply for practical reasons her parents are going to have a major planning role. Another location factor is convenience for your two families and other guests. If you're living overseas, but nearly all the people you want at your wedding are back home, then you'll have a choice to make. Not all your desired guests will be able to travel to you for the wedding, even if they'd like to.

Destination Weddings

Of course, you could have your wedding away from everyone's home base, popularly called a 'destination wedding'. I'm not talking about a wedding in wine country a two-hour drive from where you live. I'd say anything a reasonable drive or short, cheap flight away is not really a destination wedding. The classic destination wedding is held at a resort on some tropical island somewhere, and may include staying more than the weekend. In general, I'm not a champion of destination weddings because of the imposition of cost, time and inconvenience on your guests. You run a risk that some people very important to you won't be able to make it. Alternatively, some of your friends and family may come out of devotion to you, even though they can't truly afford it. But if you're loaded and happy to bear the costs of travel and accommodation for your guests, or your guest list is universally well off, then go ahead.

Despite my reservations, there are a few circumstances where a destination wedding makes particular sense:

1. *Inevitable travel.* If your families are from two different areas, then it's automatically a 'destination wedding' for one group. If the locations are far apart you might decide to hold the wedding at some place in between, such as a groom from Melbourne and a bride from North Queensland getting married in the Whitsunday Islands. In a variation on this theme, you may live away from both your families or your families and friends may be spread around, in which case your guests are going to have to travel in any respect.

2. *Small wedding.* If you're only having a small wedding with immediate family and very close friends, then you may be able to pay for their accommodation or you may be more confident that all the guests can afford the time and expense of the destination wedding.

Don't Go the Distance

Reception venue selection is discussed in the next chapter, but the ceremony and reception venue searches should be done in tandem. They both need to be available on the same date and be in the same general area. It's not always possible to find venues that are convenient to each other but it's worth the effort, especially if you can do them at the same location. Whenever human transportation is involved, there's the opportunity for mishap (just look at public transport planning in Sydney). Once we decided to have our ceremony next door to our reception venue, planning became much easier. Admittedly, this may be harder if you're fixed on a church wedding, as the church basement may not be your favoured reception venue.

As with the reception, if you're going to have the ceremony outdoors, make sure you have a *backup*. You can't count on the weather, no matter how much you pray. If God answered all the brides' prayers, we'd be in serious drought . . . oh, wait . . .

Venue Shopping

Not all houses of worship are overly welcoming to blow-in brides. It's not like booking a hotel or reception venue—the managers of religious sites answer to a higher authority than the nearly almighty dollar (a rarity in the wedding game). Be sure to phrase your enquiry as a *request* and show some tact. 'How 'bout a little something extra in the collection plate, Father' is not an acceptable approach. Still, while they don't do it for the money, there will be a fee (hey, they got to pay for cleaning all that stained glass).

CEREMONY

The ceremony can be fraught territory. Your choices may be more influenced by your families, cultures and traditions than your own beliefs and practices—it has ever been thus. You may be indifferent about the form your ceremony takes and happy to make your parents happy. On the other hand, you or your partner may have serious qualms about a religious ceremony. Even more difficult, you and your bride may come from different, but equally strong, religious backgrounds.

Let's Be Civil

The rapid growth of the civil ceremony in Australia can be traced largely to one man: Attorney-General Lionel Murphy in the time of the Whitlam government. Murphy thought the bureaucratic, registry-office wedding was debasing for couples who didn't want a religious ceremony. During his tenure (in the early 1970s), Murphy used his authority to appoint over 90 celebrants to perform civil weddings. Consequently, couples could determine their own ceremony outside of a religious structure or a clerk's office. (Amanda Lohrey's article 'A Proper Wedding' provides a good discussion of this history in the August 2009 issue of *The Monthly*.) Today, 65 per cent of Australian couples get married in civil ceremonies. This is much different to the US, where even many 'non-practising' couples get married according to their religious heritage. Of course, what the majority of Australians or Americans do has little relevance to you.

To God or Not to God

My partner and I were both raised Catholics. I was a regular churchgoer as a child, but an eventual Sunday-school dropout. While both of us consider ourselves Christian in a moral sense, neither of us is a practising Catholic. I was opposed to a Catholic wedding, largely because

PRE-CANA

Pre-Cana varies with the parish and it's always possible to find a more relaxed priest, but it generally includes a commitment to be practising Catholics and to raise your children as Catholic, which we had no intention of doing. Other Christian denominations, like the Anglican Church, may have various forms of pre-marital counselling.

of the Church's premarital requirements like *Pre-Cana*. Many couples go through the motions of their religious traditions for the sake of the ceremony they want (or their parents want). I can understand that. Most people would rather lie to God than piss off their mum (her role in your creation was a bit more direct and her wrath more imminent). In the end, we were married by a very relaxed Uniting Church minister who didn't require anything of us except what we owed to each other. So, we found a way to please God and our mums.

Divine Battle

If you and your partner are from different religious backgrounds, that can present challenges. Sometimes one partner agrees to be married according to the other's faith, and even converts. Other times it leads to joint ceremonies, or inventive ceremonies that combine religious traditions. In some instances, though, there are seemingly irreconcilable differences, if not between the couple then between their families or their faiths. Most major religions technically allow for interfaith marriages (to varying extents), but it may still cut against the cultural norms of a family's ethnic background, as when the ethnicity is culturally tied to a particular faith.

It's impossible to speak to all cases or to advise on such an intensely personal matter, but I've always admired a passage from de Tocqueville's *Democracy in America* concerning the difference between the human and divine perspective:

> Men think that the greatness of the idea of unity lies in means. God sees it in the end . . . To force all men to march in step toward the same goal—that is a human idea. To encourage endless variety of actions but to bring them about so that in a thousand different ways all tend toward the fulfilment of one great design—that is a God-given idea (de Tocqueville 1988, p. 735).

It shouldn't matter that you and your partner are on different paths to God, only that those two paths met. It's the same destination. Moreover, given that many of the world's major conflicts have centred on religious diferences, more interfaith marriage could cure many of the world's most fatal ills. It may be a struggle at times, but one worth making—if not for yourselves, then for world peace.

DOUBLE WEDDING, DOUBLE TROUBLE

I didn't think double weddings happened outside of Shakespearean comedies and soap operas, but they're mentioned in a number of wedding books. While somewhat economical, they open up a whole world of pain. Unless two sisters are marrying two brothers, we're talking about three to four sets of parents (without counting divorces and remarriages). Let's not forget about the *two brides*, either.

I don't care if they are sisters, they're each going to have their own ideas about how things should be done. As they're both 'the bride', it's like an unstoppable force meeting an immovable object—and the two grooms are sitting right in the impact zone.

It's Officiant

Whether priest, rabbi, imam or civil celebrant, your officiant is your guide for the ceremony. In addition to religious rules, traditions and customs, your officiant can educate you on the legal requirements for marriage and steer you through the logistics of your ceremony. Make sure you meet with your officiant early in the process to learn what is required of you both, the guidelines and limitations for your ceremony and the choices you have to make. Even if you use a celebrant, he or she should be able to give you some sample ceremonies, vows and readings to consider. Our minister gave us four sample ceremonies to review, ranging from very traditional to somewhat 'out there'. We chose one of the more traditional options and tweaked it to suit us.

Here are a few of the major topics you should cover when you sit down with your officiant:

1. *Religious requirements.* Particularly if one of you is marrying into the other's faith, you need to know what the rules are regarding interfaith marriage. For example, is conversion required, or any kind of pledge that the children will be raised according to the religion?

2. *Legal requirements.* Find out what is required for your marriage to be legally recognised under the laws of your state. Take careful notice of any deadlines for submitting forms, getting approvals, etc.

3. *Church a must?* Are you able to marry outside of a house of worship? Different faiths, sects and individual officiants may have different rules about this. For example, Catholic weddings are meant to take place in a Catholic church.

4. *Restrictions.* Ask what's prohibited at the ceremony site, and any limitations (e.g., for flowers, photography, video recording, music).

5. *Rehearsal.* Set a date for the rehearsal as well as the wedding (rehearsal dates book up too).

6. *Are you alone?* Find out if your ceremony venue is hosting any other weddings on the same day. It's particularly important to know if you're planning to do pictures at the site before or after your wedding or have a receiving line. That may not be possible if another wedding is arriving or still going. Also, you might be able to share the costs for flowers or other decorations with a couple having their ceremony the same day as you.

7. *Logistics.* Work out all other logistics, like parking, traffic, whether guests can throw stuff at you and any restrictions on what they can throw (apparently rice kills pigeons).

8. *Fees.* Go over any fees for use of the space and the officiant's time, as well as anything additional (organist, musical director, sexton, etc.).

The Rehearsal

Your need for a ceremony rehearsal depends on the complexity of your ceremony. A quick 'Do you?' and 'Do you?' from the Elvis impersonator in Vegas isn't going to require much forethought. A large wedding party performing intricate dance moves up the aisle is going to require some practice. Our rehearsal was brief, but very useful. None of it's rocket science, but you'll be in a weird mental space on the day so it's good to have everything mapped out for you in foolproof fashion. You can also use the rehearsal time to sort out any final particulars (such as the marriage licence).

DOG ESCORT

One bride couldn't decide between her biological or adoptive father to walk her down the aisle and came up with a unique alternative. 'Eventually I decided that my dog, Bear, would be the one to accompany me up the aisle; he also acted as my only "bridesmaid"' (Shaw 2001, p. 150). I don't know what's more messed up: that she confuses her dog with a much larger animal or that she had 'Bear' escort her down the aisle. It had to be a kick in the guts for both her fathers when they were replaced by a mutt with delusions of grandeur.

VOWS AND BLESSING

There's nothing wrong with personalising your wedding, but I want to throw out some words of warning. Not everyone is a Shakespeare, Byron, Whitman or Banjo Paterson. If you're not a wordsmith, then know your limitations. Religious wedding scripts have been used for the last few thousand years for a reason—they work. Despite their age, they manage not to be clichéd and skate that fine line between sentiment and sentimentality. It's a difficult line to walk, which you'll discover as you stare at a blank page trying to divine your own vows.

Vows

I'm just going to say it. Please, for the love of all that is good in this world, don't write your own vows. I say this because I have come across so very many bad vows. If you still feel compelled to compose your own statements of love and fidelity, let me make a few suggestions. As with all things, *brevity is key*. No one wants to hear you blabber on for ten minutes about the intricate details of your love. Next, if it sounds like a lyric from a Debbie Gibson song, then it probably is. Often, self-written vows sound like lovesick high-school students practising metaphors for English class. Just to give you an idea, stay away from the following words, phrases, sentiments and concepts (based on some *actual vows*):

1. Moonbeams, spaceships, universe, galaxy or space references of any kind.
2. Bogan language (e.g., 'I love you heaps').
3. Dragons and dragon slaying (literally or as a metaphor).
4. Any reference to sharing household chores.
5. Any reference to your shared career. Jackson Browne may have sung about 'Lawyers in Love', but vows

about the 'merger of two corporate interests' are just not on.

6. Bad, mixed or meaningless metaphors. For this, *The Smart Couple's Guide* (Shervan and Sniechowski 2005) inadvertently provides examples of what *not* to say:

- 'I promise . . . to be the joy of your heart and the food of your soul' (p. 116). It's got some good words in there, but it doesn't really mean anything.
- 'From this moment on, may our sunshine be shared' (p. 116). Was one of you previously withholding sunshine from the other?
- 'I . . . take thee . . . to be my wife . . . to the mutual benefit of all' (p. 118). Are you pimpin' out your new wife?
- 'Now I acknowledge our humanness' (p. 120). I'm so glad we got that straight.
- '[Y]ou are a treasure more laden with immensity than the sea, and you are white and blue and spacious like the earth' (p. 128). I just can't interpret that in a way where he isn't calling his bride fat. And not just a little fat—we're talking fat on a planetary scale.

Blessing

There are some great blessings out there, and that certainly isn't limited to the main religions. But if you decide to script your own blessing, I again urge you to avoid cheesy, sentimental, Hallmark greeting card crap (also courtesy of Shervan and Sniechowski 2005, p. 140):

1. '. . . intoxicate you with the miracle of who you are'—it sounds pseudo-poetic but, loosely translated, it means, 'get you drunk on your own self-absorption'.

2. '. . . embrace the lessons of the darker side' but also 'surrender to the force', which makes this sound like a wedding officiated by Yoda ('Lame, this blessing is').

3. 'And now let us take a moment to shine our joined beam of love upon Mark and Beth . . . send what is in your hearts through your eyes and smiles into their eyes and hearts and souls.' It sounds like the scene at the end of *Raiders of the Lost Ark*, when they open the ark of the covenant and beams shoot out of the bad guy's eyes and melt all the Nazis' faces. Close your eyes, Beth and Mark! Don't let the love beams melt your faces!

Readings

Even if you're restricted to religious readings, there's room to pick one that speaks to you both. If you're not so restricted, then the opportunities are endless: sonnets, lyrical passages from classic novels and even song lyrics. They're out there, just waiting to be plucked from wedding books or the World Wide Web. If you stop to think about it, there may be some passage that has special meaning for the two of you (we always get chills during Patrick Swayze's speech at the end of *Dirty Dancing*—just kidding). We used a popular Apache blessing, and I can say that neither of us had any background with Native American spirituality. Readings can also be a way to include your parents in the ceremony or other important people who didn't make the cut for the wedding party. My sister couldn't be at our wedding but we asked her to write a poem, which my mother read at the wedding.

DEAR CORINTHIANS

The most popular wedding reading from the Christian faith must be from Paul's first letter to the Corinthians: 'Love is patient and kind; love is not boastful or jealous . . .' Regrettably, every time I (or my brother) hear the reader announce 'Paul's first letter to the Corinthians', in our heads we always hear 'Dear Corinthians . . .' A struggle ensues not to burst out laughing. I know it's childish, but hey. I hope I haven't ruined that reading for you too (on the other hand, it's definitely overused).

CROSS CULTURAL

I'm all for the incorporation of your cultural traditions into your wedding. It's a great way to invest your ceremony with personal meaning (and your nanna will be totally chuffed). If you and your bride are from different cultures, you can blend traditions from both into your ceremony. It's a great way of teaching each of your families about the other. If you're looking for ideas, start by asking your families, particularly grandparents. Otherwise, online research will produce quick results.

Culture Shock

The following are a few colourful traditions that I thought worthy of mention:

1. *Mexican.* The groom hands over a dish of thirteen gold coins (or *arras*) to his bride, which symbolises giving her all his worldly possessions and his pledge to support her. That sounds more like a divorce ceremony to me—maybe we should ask Singo.

2. *Irish.* For luck, the bride used to carry an actual horseshoe with her on her wedding day. These days it's a miniature version (usually porcelain), which is good, because I don't think horseshoes featured in Christian Dior's latest accessories collection.

3. *Italian.* The men get hard liquor *before* food is served and are all meant to kiss the bride for luck, and to make the groom jealous. How does every Italian wedding not end in a knockdown, drag-out brawl? Maybe this explains another tradition: vendettas.

CHINESE TRADITION

As with Western weddings, modern Chinese weddings can have a varying combination of traditional and modern elements, but the main event is definitely the wedding banquet. In one tradition, the bride and groom visit each of the guest tables to offer a toast. The receptions are usually well attended, so the happy couple will be well and truly *toasted* before the day is through. After the wedding, the friends of the bride and groom invade the wedding suite and play silly tricks on the couple (particularly the groom) and generally hang out, smoke, drink and play mahjong until the wee hours of the morning (Chinese customs of politeness prevent the couple from turfing out the house pests).

Ang Lee's 1993 film *The Wedding Banquet* explores some of these traditions in a blend of madcappery and drama. A gay Taiwanese man living in Manhattan marries a Chinese girl to get her a green card and get himself a heterosexual alibi for his traditional parents.

Wedding Programs

When it comes to wedding programs (also called an 'order of service'), I generally say save your money. In most cases, people don't need a play-by-play of the service as they'll have seen its like before. However, if you're including traditions of your faith or culture that may not be familiar to all your guests, a program can help them follow the action and understand the *meaning* behind these traditions. Also, programs don't have to cost a lot. Like other stationery items, you can often do it yourself with a reasonable quality printer or through a copy/printing shop.

MUSIC

As with ceremonies, there are two types of music: religious and secular. Some faiths don't allow secular music to be played during the ceremony, and you have to select from the approved hymns. Of course, you can always do like Bart Simpson and sneak Iron Butterfly's seventeen-minute long 'In-A-Gadda-Da-Vidda' in front of the church organist. The song is so named because the lead singer got drunk and/or stoned one night and was slurring 'In the Garden of Eden'. At least, that's the story.

You should also check whether you have to use in-house music (e.g., church organist) or whether you can supply your own. Assuming you have the option, using the in-house folks may be simplest and cheapest unless you want one or more members of your reception band to play at the ceremony. If you do use outside musicians, make sure you ask the officiant about any restrictions (like no amplification). Of course, you can never go wrong with bagpipes. There's something about a grown Scotsman in a kilt that just screams 'wedding'.

Non-traditional Selections

Your traditional wedding books will have all the usual religious and secular musical selections for your ceremony, so I thought I would suggest some possibilities that fall somewhat off the beaten path.

1. *Prelude*: (i) 'Is She Really Going Out with Him?' (Joe Jackson), (ii) 'Somebody's Baby' (Jackson Browne—no relation) or (iii) 'Livin' on a Prayer' (Bon Jovi).
2. *Bride's processional*: (i) 'Do Wah Diddy Diddy' (Manfred Mann), (ii) 'Maneater' (Hall & Oates) or (iii) 'Walk of Life' (Dire Straits).
3. *Recessional*: (i) 'Na Na Hey Hey Kiss Him Goodbye' (Steam), (ii) 'I Ran (So Far Away)' (A Flock of Seagulls) or (iii) 'Hit the Road, Jack' (Ray Charles).

9

THE RECEPTION

*The Most Expensive Party
You'll Ever Have*

'How do we get our guests talking? Try hiring a
magician to visit the tables during dinner. You could
write humorous facts or questions about the guests
on the place-name cards'
(Love 2007, p. 53).

. . . That falls under 'Ideas So Lame They Would
Suck at a Child's Birthday Party'.

The reception is the main event, in terms of expense, planning and, hopefully, enjoyment. If couples go money crazy it's usually over the reception, and there's no need. I've been to receptions that cost a mint, others with a cash bar, and to a backyard wedding in Townsville that featured XXXX Gold in the esky. No one thought less of the backyard wedding because it wasn't in a fancy restaurant or dining hall (anyone who did could go and get stuffed). Everyone was happy for the couple, happy to be there; everyone got pissed and had a good time. You can drop $100K on a wedding (and people do), but if folks aren't having fun then what a waste. And if people are enjoying themselves, it really doesn't matter what you spend.

RECEPTION VENUE

There's no point thinking about specific reception venues until you have a vague idea about guest numbers. You don't want people crammed in like cattle class on a discount airline to Bali. Alternatively, if you have space left over for a full rugby match, it's going to feel like an empty room *and* it's a waste of money. So, get your numbers straight, then do a Goldilocks and pick something that's *just right*.

Once you figure on your size and budget, choosing the reception venue should be at the top of your 'stuff to do' list (in conjunction with picking your ceremony venue). The reception spot will lay the framework for most other decisions and will take a big bite out of the budget, also setting the boundaries for those other expenses. You may have the perfect reception venue but, if you spent too much, it's aerosol cheese and light beer for your guests.

Small Town Girl or City Boy?

If you live in a small town with few options for large events, then at least your decision is relatively simple. If none of the venues impress you there's always the great outdoors, with tents for inclement weather.

If you live in a major city or population centre, your choices of venue are going to be many—too many. When you buy a house, you don't look at everything on the market. You decide how many bedrooms you want, which neighbourhood, whether you want a yard and, most importantly, what you can afford. So, to narrow your venue search, come up with a general (and realistic) checklist. Include things like size, price, location, whether catering is included, room for band and dancing, indoor or outdoor space (or both), and so on. You should also check on site restrictions. Some places in residential areas can't have loud music or have to shut at a certain hour, and some heritage buildings won't allow dancing or high heels. In public parks, the use of tents, tables, chairs or catered food and alcohol service may be prohibited and you'll likely need a permit even to use the space. Your checklist and some research eliminates possibilities and focuses you on those places that truly meet your needs.

With a Little Help from My Friends

As with other aspects of your wedding, it's always good to ask around. Your friends may have planned their own wedding or other event in the area and their research could give you a real jump-start (we inherited a spreadsheet of Sydney venues and later passed it on to others). At the very least, your friends and family may have been to weddings and other events in the area and can give you some good ideas.

Don't get too caught up in having a truly 'unique' reception venue. The best places get used a lot, with good reason, and the managers are going to know their stuff (always helpful). Uniqueness is overrated. Having your reception at the city dump would be original, but a bit on the nose. Your reception will be unique because it will be with *your* family and *your* friends. What people remember most is the atmosphere of a wedding—how they felt when they were there. (As the sweaty lawyer said in *The Castle*, 'It's the *vibe* of the thing.') If they remember any of the little details you or your bride sweated over, like the flowers, the food or the venue, it's usually something bad. The best thing is for people to remember the good time they had (and the kickarse Journey music).

If you're planning the wedding from afar, try to have a friend or family member in the area do a check on your proposed venue, to make sure it lives up to the hype, and the photos. Airbrushing a cover model is one thing, but you don't want to base your venue decision on 30-year-old photos. (Here's a hint: if people in the background are wearing hot pants and flares, it's an old photo.)

ASPEN WEDDING RECEPTION

The Beatles say 'can't buy me love', but you can buy one hell of a reception. One slap-happy example from *The Smart Couple's Guide* is of an 'Aspen dream come true' (Shervan and Sniechowski 2005, pp. 198–200). The bride's parents were looking at a guest list of 500, but the couple talked them down to an intimate 180. The guests all flew to Aspen, the famed winter playground of the wretchedly wealthy, where each received 'a sterling-silver snowflake keepsake from Tiffany's'. They also enjoyed the musical stylings of the couple's favourite artist, Lyle Lovett, live and in person. He even signed CDs for everyone. The point of this story? If your daddy owns a gold factory you can have the perfect wedding, but you'll still be a git for liking Lyle Lovett. The same authors also shared some brilliant advice for a couple with two different ideas for their reception: 'Have two parties' (p. 202). Of course! It worked out well for everyone, including the wedding consultant, who I'm sure got a healthy cut for each party.

ROUGHING IT

It's the height of romance to stage your wedding at the perfect cliffside locale, until your bride gets hit by a stray weather balloon. If you're going to be outdoors, think about a few things:

1. Choose a time of year with good weather (avoid the monsoon season).
2. Have a backup plan, in case it pisses down on your big day.
3. Check on restrictions and necessary permissions for using a public space.
4. Make sure guests can get there without a seaplane or abseiling equipment.

We had our ceremony outside, on a little spit of harbourside sand next to our reception venue. It was sunny the entire week before our wedding and the entire week after. It rained on our wedding day, with a gusty wind that blew the bride's veil hither and thither. Fortunately, it only poured down after everyone was inside, enjoying the reception. While we had a backup plan for the ceremony (a small space under cover), I admit it would have been crowded and uncomfortable if we'd had to use it. There's a tendency to think that the universe owes you a nice wedding day, but we're just not that special and neither are you. So, think carefully about a workable backup plan.

An at-home event can be a great option for small to moderately sized weddings (family and close friends), but can be a pain for larger ones and not cost effective. Think about tents on the lawn, parking around the house, bathrooms (will you need Kenny?). For big weddings it will be simpler, if not cheaper, to hire a venue designed to cater for large groups (and God do I love simplicity).

THE MOTION IS TABLED

For the reception layout, let the venue managers be your guide. In most cases, you're going to have a venue that does events as part of their business and they'll know every layout permutation you could imagine. We held our reception at a restaurant and they gave us several floor plans, varying by number of guests, whether there was a dance floor and so on. Then it's just common-sense stuff: don't put the old folks next to the speakers, and put the singles and big drinkers' table in the back (they prefer it there anyway).

Seat Assignments

Especially for large weddings, seating assignments can be a painful process and even the most hands-off groom has to do his bit. Your partner can't know the details of every feud among your family and friends (like who slept with whom). For the same reason, letting guests fall where they may can lead to awkwardness and a bit of chaos when it's time to sit down. It's hard enough pulling people from the bar at meal time. A good compromise is to assign people to tables, but not individual seats. It's a common approach, and the one we took. It saves a large portion of pain (we did the table assignments quickly and with minimal fuss) and provides a nice balance between order and flexibility.

The King's Table

Etiquette has a blueprint for seating at the wedding table: the best man is to the right of the bride and the maid of honour sits to the left of the

> **IT'S NOT GYMBOREE**
>
> When arranging the seating, *do not* make your reception a forced social mixer: this is not an industry conference, the first day at kindy or a Scientology meeting. Some couples think of their reception as a 'get to know you' opportunity, splitting up family and friends, even seating couples at different tables. Don't do this. You want your guests to enjoy themselves, and they'll do that best if they're with the people they know best (in some cases, people they don't get to see too often). Inevitably, not everyone at every table is going to know each other, so guests meet a few new people anyway. The exception to the rule is the set-up. It's always fine (and fun) to throw a few tables of mixed singles together to see what happens (see 'The Meat Market Game' box in Chapter 5).

groom. We did it the other way. I wanted my brother next to me, especially as he had flown a long way to be there. Likewise, my bride wanted her sister by her side. Use the wedding book arrangement as your guide, but do what makes sense for you.

Do you include partners of your wedding party at the wedding table? I feel funny about splitting up couples but, with a large wedding party, adding partners to the table may not be practical. We only had a best man and maid of honour, so we included their spouses at the table. However, some of you crazy kids will have massive wedding parties that include every relative and every friend since preschool (except those who owe you money).

Assuming there's still room at the table, parents are another question, which can be further complicated by divorce. Here's a bold idea: rather than consulting the

SUFFER THE CHILDREN

Some wedding books talk about a special playroom and hiring a magician for the kiddies. To me, a wedding ain't a kids' birthday party, and while it's nice to do you shouldn't feel compelled to incur those costs. Besides, kids can keep themselves entertained with much less. Consider some activity bags or plop them in front of a DVD (TV will be raising them mostly, anyway). Otherwise, suggest a good game of 'pin the tail on the bridesmaid' (if your grooms-men aren't already at it), which could add greatly to your entertainment as well.

wedding books, talk to your parents about where they want to sit. Their thoughts on the matter seem more relevant than those of some self-appointed etiquette mogul you've never met. Just be considerate and don't force estranged parents to sit together for the sake of appearances, (this isn't *The Parent Trap*). You want them to enjoy themselves too and minimise any tension.

GET UP, GET ON UP

If you don't want to do a formal sit-down reception, there are several other options that offer a freer flow for the day. Also consider the timing of your reception and relative costs. Evening receptions tend to be more formal, which generally means more expensive (i.e., they don't serve spam and generic cola at black-tie weddings).

Buffet

A buffet can be a good option and is especially suited to brunch and lunch receptions and less formal venues, like a private home. Interestingly, a buffet is not necessarily cheaper than a seated meal, as the necessary quantity of each food type cannot be precisely foreseen. The benefit is maximum choice for guests and they can also come back for more. It works especially well if you're after a more casual flow, where guests can move around and talk to different people more easily.

Cocktail

A cocktail reception, with passed trays of finger food, is another less structured option. Again, guests are not confined to tables and can mingle more freely. Cocktail receptions also tend to be cheaper than buffets or sit-downs. However, a serious word of caution: if the reception is crossing a meal time (as it most likely will), make sure some substantial food is served. Getting people liquored up and not providing real food is a recipe for disaster (think of your last office Christmas party). If your friends or rellies are known for telling folks what they *really* think of them when they get stuck into the piss, your wedding day could end in tears without some pass-around pasta and hefty meatballs on sticks.

TUCKER AND GROG

Your big advantage on reception tucker is that no one really expects it to be good (ah, low expectations—every man's best friend in a relationship). People know that places where food is made en masse (schools, the military, prisons and business conferences) are not known for their culinary excellence. So, it becomes hard to disappoint. If you manage to have better than average food, people will be pleasantly surprised.

Drop the Alternate Drop

One of the 'discussions' I had with my blushing bride was over 'alternate drop' food service. This may be one of those deep crevices in the Aussie–Yank divide, because the idea is just weird to me: a guest's meal is a lottery based on where he or she sits. People can always switch around, I'm told, and that's a great image: guests trading salmon and lamb chops like schoolkids with pudding packs. I understand that to save costs the caterers need to know how many chooks to throttle and cows to butcher, but why not have guests choose their meal when they RSVP to the wedding? Then they get something of their choosing instead of dropped something they may hate, and the caterers will still know exactly what to cook up.

COMMON DENOMINATORS

Your reception is not the time to foist your unique palate on your guests. Shoot for the lowest common denominators, like chicken, beef, salmon and lamb. If you really want to include an exotic dish, especially if it reflects your ethnic background or heritage, that's fine, but include some staple options as well. Venues should also offer a vegetarian choice, though you will probably need to let the caterers know in advance on the number of tree munchers.

Another odd approach is 'duet service', where everyone gets two different meals on one plate. That's great for hungry folks who happen to like both (nothing wrong with a little surf and turf), but the actual idea is to make sure that everyone likes at least one of the offerings, which assumes that most people will only eat half their plate. Maybe it's my mother's voice talking about the starving kids in Bangladesh, but that seems damn wasteful to me and expensive.

Just have your guests choose ahead of time—simpler, cheaper and everybody's happy. If choice is really important to you, you can go with a restaurant venue, as we did. They're better equipped to give your guests different menu options on the day (a selection of three entrees and three mains came with our package).

Drink and Be Married

The bar may be of particular interest to you. If cost is a concern you can limit the open bar to beer and wine, with champagne for toasting (for per bottle vs per head costing, see 'Wedding Contracts' in Chapter 7. This may also be a way of limiting the drunkenness to a spirited yet manageable level, especially if your friends or family have been known to bring out the riot police. The etiquette books say you can never let anyone pay for anything, but if you've got a beer and wine bar and some guest is happy to pay for spirits, I don't see the point in prohibiting it. Having a BYO whiskey policy is probably a bit cheeky, but I'm not going to judge you or your guests.

Couples will sometimes throw a few special cocktails into the mix, but this is usually mimosas, bellinis, cosmos and other *Sex and the City* crap, so 'car bombs' for your mates is probably out. You may also want to consider special orders; we had to get a case of XXXX Gold for the North Queenslanders in my bride's family.

Review and Swallow

If you get the chance to do a tasting with your bride, jump on it. You get to try a bunch of different food and get credit for 'being involved'—that's a try and a conversion. A beer-tasting request is probably pushing it. Don't forget to sample the wines too. We didn't like our initial selection (the restaurant let us sample a bottle) and switched to one we much preferred. Again, people are not expecting fantastic wine for a wedding, but it's nice to have something that goes down well and roughly matches the food you've chosen. Also, consider that many people these days (myself included) have a distaste for chardonnay and merlot, two common choices for weddings. Think about going a different way (a riesling or sav blanc and a pinot, which tends to go well with everything) or consider having a couple of options, assuming it doesn't cost more.

Have Your Cake (and Eat it Too)

Cleary, there's an international cabal of wedding professionals who meet every year and invent new crap for people to spend money on. Someone sits up front, stroking a white cat, and blurts out 'calligraphy', 'bonbonnière' or 'monogrammed toasting glasses'. The word is given and wedding planners, book writers, magazine editors and bloggers the world over make them the new 'must-haves' of the wedding season. I'm fairly sure this is how the groom's cake (a second cake that more reflects the groom's tastes) was born.

That said, there's few things in the wedding with the groom's name on it, so if you want to grab on to this one fair enough. If you're getting the traditional, white frosted wedding cake, you may want to have a heavier, chocolate alternative, which is popular for a groom's cake. Or, you could

> **RECURRING THEME**
>
> You'll notice a recurring theme in this book: don't do anything that would be done at a child's birthday party (theme cakes, magician, clown, piñata, pin the tail on the drunk uncle, etc.). It's a good wedding rule to live by.

just have an alternative dessert. In another burst of cost-enhancing creativity, the wedding industry suggests having the groom's cake reflect one of your interests or hobbies (like a rugby cake), but that sounds a bit too much like something your parents did for your twelfth birthday party.

ASSAULT BY CHOCOLATE

There's a wedding tradition in which the bride and groom simultaneously hand feed each other the first bite of wedding cake. I'm sure it's symbolic of nourishing their lives together, or some junk like that. Some larrikin newlyweds take this opportunity to playfully smash the cake into their partner's face. That may sound like some light-hearted hijinks to you but, according to *The Smart Couple's Guide*, it's a criminal act: 'we have heard far too many stories of husbands or wives surprising their mates with a face full of frosting . . . This is not funny. It is abuse—and it is publicly condoned abuse at that, when guests laugh and applaud' (Shervan and Sniechowski 2005, p. 182). So, if you don't want to spend your wedding night in the local lock-up, you better take this cake business seriously lest an errant bit of frosting on the cheek gets you done for assault.

HE BEGAN TO SUSPECT HE'D CHOSEN THE <u>WORST</u> MAN...

10

THE BEST MAN

And Other Hangers On

On being asked to be best man: *'Once the initial thrill of the good news has sunk in, the feeling of being honoured . . . gradually wears off and the most common reaction is one of blind panic . . . How will I cope?'* (Bryant 2005, p. 7).

. . . I'm sorry, but men don't react this way. We are not *thrilled*, we do not have *feelings* and we do not *panic* about fulfilling ceremonial duties with minimal requirements.

CO-BEST MEN

In a poignant episode of *Scrubs*, Turk has to make a painful best man decision between his brother and his best friend, JD, who's like a brother from another mother. This led to 'co-best men', which was a bit of a TV cop-out, but whatever works for you.

The traditional wedding books say that your groomsmen should be people you can talk to about your feelings and emotions. But guys are like Vulcans: we don't have 'feelings' or 'emotions' (or if we do, we certainly don't *talk* about them). Instead, your groomsmen should be mates you can grab a beer and chat with about all the crap you have to deal with for this wedding.

Selection of a best man can be relatively straightforward. If you have one brother and you don't hate him, that's pretty much the go. Otherwise, there can be some careful politics (like choosing between brothers or friends), and then there are the groomsmen. Still, it's not the hair-pulling, friendship-ending calamity of choosing bridesmaids. Most blokes won't be slighted if they don't make it in the top three or four of your very bestest friends.

CHOOSING YOUR TEAM

If you have a brother he should probably be your first choice for best man, even if he's hopeless. Not choosing him can be a slight, without good reason (e.g., he's currently doing time). It can also lead to general family strife. Any mate who gets passed over for a brother will understand, and if your mate is really the better best man he can be slipped some best man duties under the table. We're just talking about what goes on the wedding program. If you have two or more brothers the default may be the oldest, but feel free to pick whomever you're closest to.

Choosing among friends for best man and groomsmen is less obvious. One way is to have a representative from different times of your life, like a childhood friend, a school friend and a work friend. Be sure to select groomsmen who will look out for you, run interference and take care of things you don't want to deal with on the wedding day. They are your entourage—your physical and mental bouncers, keeping out the literal and metaphorical bogans. They also need to take care of you (in the good way) when you've overindulged on your bucks' night (not losing you in Vegas, like in the 2009 film *The Hangover*).

Feats of Strength

One groom had a brilliantly innovative idea for choosing his groomsmen: a test of skill. He planned a round robin tennis tournament with sixteen competitors. You can choose whatever form of physical or mental combat that suits you (poker tournament, bowling, Ultimate Fighting cage-match showdown). It can be rolled quite nicely into a bucks'

> **FESTIVUS**
>
> 'Feats of Strength' takes place at the conclusion of the Festivus holiday, invented by Frank Costanza (George's father) on *Seinfeld*. Festivus isn't over until the head of the household is pinned in a wrestling match by a challenger of his choosing. Festivus also features the 'Airing of Grievances', in which 'you gather your family around, and tell them all the ways they have disappointed you over the past year'—something to be avoided in the wedding toasts.

weekend. The winner of the contest becomes your best man, and the second, third, etc. in the tally are your groomsmen. This harkens back to days of yore, when groomsmen provided armed protection for the groom as he kidnapped his bride from a neighbouring village (that was romance in the 12th century). In that case, you'd want someone handy with a tennis racket to say the least.

The best thing about this approach is: no hard feelings. You don't have to rank your brothers or friends in importance—they do that themselves. As few wedding decisions are wholly yours, don't leave the groomsmen decision to your family, your bride or even your own careful consideration. Leave it to an arbitrary test of skill.

They Say Yes, I Say No

More than one groom advice book suggests your father as best man. I guess that's sweet, if you're close with your old man, but I think it's kinda weird. Your best man should really be a contemporary. It's particularly creepy as the best man is meant to organise the bucks' night. Maybe my dad goes to strip clubs, I don't know . . . and I don't want to know, much less witness a paternal lap dance. Nor could my father fully appreciate the subtle nuances of *Harold & Kumar Go to White Castle*, a favourite film from my bucks' weekend. Your dad has a role in the wedding—as father of the groom. If you want to include him more, he can wear a wedding tux and a boutonniere thingy, just like the groomsmen.

Even worse is the galactically stupid idea of a groomswoman. It's nice that wedding etiquette has loosened up enough to allow this, but it's a very bad idea for you. A female groom's attendant is unusual, so it gets noticed. Now a woman is getting noticed who is not the bride. A woman's wedding day is the one day in her life when she is indisputably the sole centre of attention, if not all creation, and you and your wingwoman have just jeopardised that (Why do you think bridesmaids' dresses have been so ugly and ill-fitting through the ages?).

Sound smart? No, it doesn't. Even stupider is if you choose a 'friend' or, worse, an 'ex' for your entourage, in which case I doubt your wedding makes it to the chapel. You might get by with a sister or cousin, but even if it's a lifetime platonic friend that you've never been attracted to your bride probably harbours some secret doubt about her in the dark, jealous, back recesses of her mind. Besides, she's seen *When Harry Met Sally* half a dozen times and accepts as male orthodoxy that we all want to sleep with our female friends.

You know your bride better than me. If she wears Birkenstocks, champions the rights of 'womyn' and is on a mission to overthrow all social conventions, then go ahead and have a groomswoman, get married by a Mayan medicine man and have the guests toss lentils at you. Otherwise, make sure there's only *one* woman standing next to you on your wedding day.

MALE ORTHODOXY

Harry: Because no man can be friends with a woman that he finds attractive. He always wants to have sex with her.
Sally: So, you're saying that a man can be friends with a woman he finds unattractive?
Harry: No. You pretty much want to nail them too.

People You Don't Have to Pick

While it's a nice thing to do, neither the bride nor the groom should feel pressure to include their partner's sibling in the wedding party. So you don't have to ask her brother, especially if he's a complete wanker. If it's a matter of excluding a good mate or having more groomsmen than you wanted, there should be no hard feelings.

A HANGOVER PROMISE

In the instant classic *The Hangover*, the groom's well-meaning future brother-in-law, Alan, promises to reveal nothing of the impending Las Vegas bucks' trip . . . including if they happen to kill someone.

Also, if your future brother-in-law is in the wedding party he has to be invited to the bucks' night. Although he's a man, and he knows men are men, his first loyalty is to his sister, so he may not fully appreciate all the hijinks and general bally-who of your bucks' festivities. There's even a chance he'll report back to your bride (though that would be a really dick move, assuming you didn't kill or sleep with anyone).

You also don't have to pick someone because you were a groomsman in his wedding. First, you may have a smaller wedding party than he did. Second, his wedding may have been a while ago and you may not be as close any more. Third, he may *like* you like you, but you just like him (unrequited bromance). Finally, he may owe you money, and that just makes things weird.

There are always secondary honours for friends who don't make the wedding party cut, like the MC, readers at the service and ushers. Just don't create make-work roles (it's a wedding, not an economic stimulus program). Some supposed 'honours' mentioned in wedding books just sound made up (e.g., guest-book attendant, coordinating photos with the photographer, serving cake, pouring tea and coffee). That's stuff that should be done either by the wedding party or, more appropriately, paid help. Valet parking attendant is an 'honour role' the same way a cleaner is a 'maintenance engineer', and you shouldn't expect either to work for free.

HONORARY ATTENDANTS

The wedding authorities say you can give people 'honourable mention' by listing them as an attendant in name only in the wedding program. Though normally reserved for people who cannot attend the wedding, it's also used as a second prize for those who missed the cut. In either case, this betrays a greatly overblown perception of the honour that you're bestowing on people by putting them in your wedding party. It's not the Victoria Cross, so don't hand out fake titles like you're Queen Elizabeth.

LABOURS

Being a best man or groomsman isn't all beer and skittles and bucks' nights. Here's the lowdown on the tasks you can ask your entourage to perform.

Best Man Duties

In olden times, the best man was a single lad who married the bride if the groom didn't show. If you have a well-sought-after bride, I'm not sure you want to invest your best man with that kind of authority. It creates bad incentives. Here are some more modern best man tasks:

1. *Arse out of bed.* The best man's most important job is to make sure you get out of bed, shower (use soap), get dressed (fully and properly) and get your arse to the wedding *early*, without stopping at the pub or hopping on an impromptu flight to Guam. Remembering crucial things like the rings is also key.

2. *Handler.* You want someone who can handle you if you totally lose the plot—someone who can kick you in the arse. That's a mate. Notorious, unrelenting drunks should be excluded (the toast alone is reason enough). An alcoholic's promise of good behaviour, however genuine, cannot be trusted.

3. *Captain of the guard.* The best man is your head groomsman. He helps you coordinate them for their few responsibilities, like getting fitted for a tux and when to be where. You might bring him along to pick out the tuxes or include him on other groomsmen decisions. Just don't hold hands while you shop.

4. *Slap around the head.* An important pre-wedding job is to tell you to cave on stuff when you're arguing with your bride. He should remind you that: (1) this is her day, and (2) you don't really care about the font on the name cards.

5. *Bucks' night.* Obviously, your best man is the chief planner and coordinator of your bucks' night. There's much more on the bucks' night in Chapter 13.

6. *The toast.* The toast is the most prominent best man duty. Guidance for all toasts is provided in Chapter 14.

7. *Bag man.* You're likely to be a bit stupid on your wedding day (happens to the best of us), so let your best man be your bag man. Organise any payments to be made on the day (e.g., the officiant, the band, the driver, tips) and put them in marked envelopes. Hand them to the best man, with instructions, and let him look after it. You might want to give him some reserve cash too, in case you forgot anything or something unexpected comes up.

8. *Transport.* Traditionally, the best man arranged transport for the groom and groomsmen as well as the couple's transport from the wedding to the reception and from the reception to the hotel, which could include doing some driving himself. These days it's more common for the couple to coordinate transport, but you can always call on the best man to be part of the plan (maybe give you a ride to the wedding, or pick up Grandma Mabel from the airport).

9. *Emergencies.* You and (mostly) your bride have spent months planning your wedding, so on the actual day you shouldn't have to deal with any bullshit. If there are any emergencies, like the unexpected arrival of your evil twin, let the best man handle it. He should also help keep the day on schedule, especially if he's doubling as the MC.

FAKE QUESTION, REAL ANSWER

Q: What's the difference between a 'groomsman' and an 'usher'?

A: Usually, nothing. In most cases, ushering is just one of the glamorous duties performed by groomsmen. In larger weddings you may have one or more ushers in addition to groomsmen whose sole job is to usher. They don't stand with you at the altar (if they do, that really makes them groomsmen) and they may or may not be dressed up like your groomsmen or be in the wedding party photos (that's up to you).

Groomsmen Duties

1. *Arrival.* Groomsmen are your people movers. They arrive early, hand out programs (aka orders of service), tell guests any rules and restrictions of the venue (no cheesy band t-shirts), help direct people to parking and answer questions (timing, taxi services, location of bathrooms or bar, the atomic weight of cobalt).

2. *Ushering.* Your groomsmen/ushers show guests to their seats (groom's on the right and bride's on the left, but there should be balanced numbers between the two sides). They should know where key family members are meant to sit and help any older or disabled guests. Instruct them to put all babies and small children under 'cones of silence' like the ones used in *Get Smart*—if only, but stick them in the

back—and to seat thoughtless latecomers quietly in obstructed-view seating. In formal weddings, a woman is 'escorted' (arm in arm) to her seat while her date walks behind, but I wouldn't try that with burly boyfriends who look out of step with wedding ushering niceties. The last official seating is the mother of the bride to the front pew, escorted by the best man or 'chief usher'. That's the gunshot start for the ceremony.

3. *Standing.* Your groomsmen stand next to you during the ceremony and try not to fidget, smirk, giggle or look down the dress of any bridesmaid (there's a time and place—and that's the reception).

4. *Departure.* This is arrival in reverse. Groomsmen help guests get from the church to the reception (offering directions, lifts, taxis) and pick up any stray programs or left property at the ceremony.

5. *Reception.* This is Arrival II. Groomsmen direct people at the reception venue, help organise the receiving line (where guests queue up to formally and briefly greet the bride, groom and their parents on their way in—done at more formal weddings), get drinks and/or canapés for people waiting in the receiving line, etc. During (and after) the reception, they also keep the bridesmaids entertained.

General Duties

1. *Dancing.* Traditionally, the maid of honour is supposed to dance with all the groomsmen at the wedding, which makes her a bit of a floozy. I think

the best man and/or whatever groomsman she may have the hots for would be sufficient. The best man is supposed to do the same, but these rules stem from a time when the wedding party were all single. The best man (and the groomsmen) should probably shy away from bridesmaids with large husbands or boyfriends. Not mowing another man's grass is more powerful etiquette, with heavier enforcement.

2. *Communications.* The best man, maid of honour, MC and other principal figures should all have each other's mobile numbers. Neither you nor the bride should be fielding calls on the wedding day. Give your phone to the best man and she can give hers to the maid of honour (I don't know where a bride would stick a phone, anyway). If something goes wrong or there are delays, the best man and groomsmen should be able to get in touch with the father of the bride, the maid of honour and the brides-maids, and vice versa. Just remember to set all phones to vibrate once inside the church.

> **SEX AND THE CRAZY**
>
> If the crazy lady and Mr Big in the *Sex and the City* movie had better communications on their wedding day, it would have spared me the last 35 minutes of that excruciatingly painful viewing experience—not my choice, believe me.

PREPARATION

Like villains in spy movies, your wedding party members 'require *information*'. Be sure to keep them abreast of your wedding plans, particularly things that affect them.

Threads

Dressing your groomsmen is pretty straightforward: they simply follow you in suit. If you wear a tux, they wear a tux. If you wear a dark suit, they wear a dark suit. If you're having an underwater ceremony, they slip on the scuba gear. If you're going the tux route, it will usually be rentals and you'll pick it all out. You can make your tux stand out a little with a different colour vest or tie; that's all up to you (if your bride lets it be). A friend of Scottish descent had his wedding vest made from his family tartan cloth—a nice touch.

The fathers may dress to your level as well, in which case they should roughly match you and the groomsmen. If you have ushers in addition to groomsmen, they can be dressed the same as the groomsmen or a step down (for example, the groomsmen in tuxes and the ushers in dark suits). Tux rentals aren't cheap, so if you can save your ushers a few bob it's nice if they can skip it. You can make them stand out with a boutonniere thingy—no man wears a flower unless it's a matter of duty.

Any out-of-town groomsmen who can't make it to a fitting should send in their measurements for the tux rental. Make sure they aren't guessing—they should pop into their local tailor and get measurements taken. It's very hard to make adjustments if they're arriving shortly before the wedding.

Backups and Smack-downs

If you have an attendant back out, can you get a replacement? If it's last minute, wardrobe matters may make this difficult. Regardless, this isn't a beauty pageant, so it's a little funny to ask a 'runner-up' for groomsman to step in. It's probably best to go with a man down. There's no law that says you have to have the exact same number of bridesmaids and groomsmen (you can tell your bride that symmetry is not a law, it's an aesthetic). It's certainly less hassle than scrambling for a wedding tux.

The New Book of Wedding Etiquette (which must have been 'new' in about 1854) addresses the perilous situation of a bridesmaid so intransigent that she must be given the sack. Such a person simply 'does not treat you with the deference and kindness that you think should be afforded' (Shaw 2001, p. 73) to what is assuredly an insanely demanding bride. Australian law does not formally require two written warnings before firing a wedding attendant, but there's still the matter of severance. If the attendant is out of pocket (for a tux rental or dress), it's probably best to front up.

It's unlikely that you'll have to sack a groomsman; it's not a demanding job and hard to foul up. However, massive bucks' night indiscretions have been known to force the issue. Fortunately, *The New Book* has a script for firing bridesmaids (pp. 73–4) that I've translated for use with a wayward groomsman:

THE NEW BOOK	TRANSLATION
'I've noticed that my choosing you to be in my wedding has really caused some problems between us.'	Ever since I asked you to be a groomsman, you've been a complete prick.

THE NEW BOOK	TRANSLATION
'I know we don't spend time together like we used to, and that's why I thought it would be fun for you to be in the wedding . . .'	I know we haven't hung out in a while but, seriously, when did you become such a prick?
'. . . but if it's causing you stress, I'll understand if you'd rather come as a guest'.	So suck it up, quit being such a prick, or step to the back of the receiving line.

OTHER STUFF

Here are a few final tidbits.

Wedding Party Gifts

Gifts for the wedding party are a nice thing to do, but not necessary (again, think about your budget). Before you go splurging on silver Tiffany corn holders (I rarely use mine), consider using that cash to defer the *costs* of being a wedding attendant. Pay for the tux rental, for example. That will be truly appreciated. If you and your bride are set on giving gifts, then make it something personal or connect it to the wedding. A group spa treatment for the girls is nice, and you can shout the boys a round of golf or a day at the footy.

The Kiddies

I have little advice to offer on child wedding attendants. They can be adorable. Of course, they can also trip, freak out, get a case of the giggles, run to their parents or have snot bubbles popping out of their nose.

My nephew, who was two at the time, insisted on featuring in his parents' wedding. He looked quite precious in his tux, but when the time came he had a little freak-out and ran to his dad (the groom) to be held, where he remained throughout the ceremony. He refused to go to anyone else and there isn't a photo of him where he isn't sucking on the end of his blankie. So, like WC Fields, you may decide to 'never work with children or animals'. It's a thin line between cute and snot.

11

THE WEDDING
CONSIGLIERE

All the Queen's Horses and
All the Queen's Women

*'I can't believe it. You make someone a bridesmaid
and they shit all over you'*
(Ginny Baker, *Sixteen Candles*).

. . . Is there anything *Sixteen Candles* didn't
teach us about life?

WARTIME CONSIGLIERE

'Consigliere' is a reference to the Godfather's principal adviser, played by Robert Duvall in the first two *Godfather* films. In a wedding situation, your bride will definitely want a 'wartime consigliere'. Hopefully, she's somewhat more attractive and friendly than Duvall. You don't want to end up with a bloody horse's head between the sheets because you forgot to pay the deposit on the reception venue.

Whether it be her mother, sister, friend, wedding planner or some Voltron combination, most brides have a principal female wedding adviser or 'wedding consigliere'. The wedding consigliere can be quite helpful, in that she gives your bride someone else to speak to regarding the many, many wedding details that you'd rather not know about. On the other hand, the groom may find himself at odds with the wedding consigliere on some aspect of the wedding, and that can be a delicate and dangerous situation.

Beyond the consigliere is the rest of the bridal retinue, including her flock of bridesmaids and other female cohorts. They will shower your bride with wedding magazines, advice, ideas, horror stories and . . . well . . . showers. In a way, the less you know about this taffeta nightmare the better. However, I've assembled a few bits of knowledge I deemed useful, if not necessary, for the groom to know about the bride's side of the wedding party.

SIZE MATTERS (AGAIN)

The size of your wedding largely determines the size of your wedding party (just logic). Don't go nuts, and try to keep your bride from going nuts too (a tougher proposition).

There are weddings with a ridiculous number of attendants, and it becomes an unholy pain in the arse. My bride had been a bridesmaid numerous times, so she was over the whole thing. She was not looking forward to picking a dress that looked good on women of different shapes, sizes and complexions (which is impossible, unless you have bridesmaids from *Children of the Corn*). So, we went simple and just had a maid of honour (her sister) and a best man (my brother).

SNOW WHITE AND THE SEVEN BRIDESMAIDS

Once upon a time, Snow White chose her five bridesmaids: her only sister, the groom's sister and three close friends. Then Snow's mother put pressure on her to add her two younger cousins, Flurry and Sleety, to whom Snow was not especially close. The advice of the wedding professional? 'The answer is easy: You must include your cousins' (Shaw 2001, p. 59). My response is easy too: screw that.

If there's one thing you and your partner should choose *without interference*, it's who's standing beside you on your wedding day. Snow was gracious enough to include the groom's sister. It's not right to foist her cousins on her who, by the way, may have no interest in being bridesmaids. This would stick Snow with *seven* bridesmaids—a whole bloody netball team. It's hard enough to find a dress that makes three women happy, let alone seven (particularly if some are netballers).

There are no required numbers and no requirement of symmetry, though your bride may feel differently. Brides often want more bridesmaids than grooms want groomsmen. Sometimes there are even two girls for every boy, like the song says. Groomsmen rarely complain.

ATTENDANT EXPENSES

You and your bride should be conscious of the financial burdens that you're asking your wedding party to bear. Remember that men and women in their twenties and early thirties are sometimes asked to be in several weddings a year. You should also be upfront with your crew about those expenses. As a bridesmaid, my partner was often in the dark about what she was expected to pay for. One heavy wedding year, my partner was going through her finances and couldn't figure out why she hadn't saved more money. She realised that a major factor was all the weddings she'd attended as a bridesmaid. The flights, hotel, hair, shoes, make-up, jewellery and the dreaded dress really add up.

This isn't as much of an issue for the boys, but they still have some costs. They can include transportation and accommodation (which any out-of-town guest faces), as well as tux and shoe rental for a more formal wedding. For both groomsmen and bridesmaids, that's not to mention shower and engagement gifts, wedding gifts and hens' and bucks' nights.

Who Pays for What

According to etiquette, a couple arranges or pays for accommodation for the wedding party (and, if generous, their transportation), but the wedding party pays for their outfits. This doesn't make a lot of sense. First, accommodation and transport costs are common to all out-of-town wedding guests, so they've got nothing to do with being in the wedding party. Second, you're giving a big benefit to your out-of-town attendants but nothing for the locals, who won't have accommodation or transportation costs. If you're going to pick up the tab on something, it should be the outfits or other expenses related to an attendant's role in the wedding. That way everyone in the wedding party gets the same benefit.

You can pay the rental fee for your groomsmen's tuxes (I paid for my brother's tux). My partner was in a wedding where the bride had a designer friend make the dresses, which made them expensive, so the bride paid half the cost. In the end, I don't think it matters too much *what* you pay for. What matters is that you're conscious of the expenses and that you contribute in some meaningful way, particularly if they're beyond the norm. Just remember to *factor those costs into your budget*. Many couples realise late in the day what the costs are going to be for their attendants and only then decide to pay for some of it. That will be a hit to your budget if you didn't anticipate the expenditure (which is also why you have a reserve—see Chapter 6).

Another possibility is to make it clear that attendants are not to get you any engagement, shower or wedding gifts (i.e., their service as your attendant and corresponding expenses are their gifts to you), especially if you're already going to get more gifts than you possibly need.

PICKING BRIDESMAIDS (AND THEIR DRESSES)

Why on earth am I telling you about bridesmaids and their dresses? Fair question. It has to do with the reflective properties of wedding stress. Essentially, if your bride is really stressed that stress will inevitably affect you in negative ways, making *you* stressed. Your stress, in turn, gets her more stressed, until you both find yourselves trapped in some horrible wedding stress echo chamber of hell. (The 'horrible wedding stress echo chamber of hell' has been trademarked and a patent application is pending for use in questioning terrorism suspects.) So it's important to have a vague understanding of her main stress-inducers—bridesmaids, and particularly their dresses, are high on the list.

No Fat Chicks

As bad as men can be, women (particularly mothers) can be ten times worse, as in this heartwarming tale. Ugly Betty wrote to a wedding etiquette specialist to enquire whether she should turn down an offer to be a bridesmaid because, in her own loving mother's view, she was 'overweight' (Post 2006, p. 78). The specialist assured Betty that being a bridesmaid is not about looks, and she should accept the honour 'with love and happiness'. The etiquette lady left out the part where Ugly Betty should tell her mother to go jump. Besides, there's nothing worse for a bride than to have five Kate Mosses standing by her side.

Pregnant Bridesmaids

My mother wasn't the matron of honour at her sister's wedding because she was far along in her pregnancy, and that simply wasn't done in those days. Happily, that kind of hyper-puritanical stigma of pregnancy has faded and women are no longer forced into 'confinement' as far as the wedding party goes. In our wedding, my bride's sister was very obviously pregnant but she was still the maid of honour. Fortunately, times and standards change.

> **MATRONLY**
>
> Technically, as a married woman my bride's sister was the 'matron of honour', but I think referring to any woman as 'matron' makes them want to punch you, and the last thing you want to do is piss off a pregnant lady (though that's a whole other book). I think it's best if we dump the 'matron' moniker and make all bridal attendants maids again for the wedding day.

Bridesmaid Dresses

Picking a dress that suits every bridesmaid is largely impossible (which usually means a dress that suits none of them). There's also stress over the cost of the dress and accessories that your bride is either imposing on her friends or adding to your budget, along with the logistics of getting everyone fitted, especially out-of-towners. Most importantly, it opens up massive avenues for dispute between your bride and her bridesmaids. It probably won't be a proper dust-up, like us boys have, so you might not recognise it. It will involve suppressed and seething anger manifested through many behind-the-back, bitter, undermining remarks fired off in multiple directions. Whatever form it takes, it means stress for your bride and thus *trouble for you*.

There may be a glimmer of hope. Apparently, it's now okay for the bridesmaid dresses to differ from each other.

Your bride could select a general type of dress (like the fabric and colour), but have each bridesmaid pick from several styles (e.g., full-length, knee-length, long or short sleeves). Alternatively, your bride could give some general criteria (light blue, floor-length, v-neck) and let the bridesmaids pick any dress that fits the general description.

This is a great innovation in wedding stress reduction. Each bridesmaid gets to pick a dress that suits her and her budget, and she might even be able to wear it again. Also, out-of-towners don't have to worry about travelling to town for fittings. Most importantly, it saves your bride the stress of making the hard decision and dealing with the fallout among her closest friends. So, you may want to suggest this option to your bride, noting its current acceptability (it should say so in her wedding books too). Of course, she may come back with any of the following:

1. 'But I want my bridesmaids wearing the *same* dress. That's how I always pictured it.'
2. 'It's important to have symmetry. You wouldn't understand.'
3. 'It's not that simple. You can't just *fix* everything, you know.'

Well, you tried. It's best to back away slowly and go to the pub. Maybe later you can make her some herbal tea and give her a back rub.

CATFIGHT

Women have an intimacy in their friendships that we will never know with our mates. They share the confidence of priest, doctor and therapist (including sex therapist). It's also true that when two good women friends live together, it can mean the end of their friendship. Likewise, a bridal party can easily end in tears. I hear more stories of tension and dispute between women in the midst of wedding arrangements than at any other time. It's partly the dress and related craziness, but the bridesmaids may also feel like they are losing one of their best friends, in a way. At the very least, that sense of intimacy they shared, sometimes since childhood, will be diminished (like it or not, you are her principal confidant now, on things about which you were once blissfully ignorant). Sometimes, when we're losing a friend, it's easier to have a stoush than to deal with it. Remember when you were eight and your best friend was moving away, so you picked a fight with him because that was easier than saying goodbye? Well, there you go.

You want to be a hero? When your bride starts getting all out of sorts with her bridesmaids, get her to think about it from their perspective. She may yell at you for taking their side. She may stare at you in dumbstruck awe, never expecting such insight into female emotional territory from the lips of men. Or, she may think you're gay and suggest you get a script-writing job on the next *Sex and the City* movie. In any event, the last place you want to be in a catfight is between the cats. At the end of the day, you have to be in your bride's corner. Just make it a far, back corner away from the flying claws and gnashing of teeth.

Human Barbie Dolls

> There have been brides who have told attendants to lose weight, have teeth capped, hold off getting pregnant, or undergo skin treatments before the wedding (Post 2006, p. 259).

Your wedding is not an audition for *Australia's Next Top Model* (though if it were, you'd spend a lot less on food). Frankly, I don't know why you'd want to marry a woman who would make those kinds of demands of her relatives and best friends because, let's face it, *you're next*. It won't be long

BRIDESMAID CONTRACT

Some brides are so controlling that they ask their bridesmaids to sign a *contract* covering their appearance, responsibilities, attendance at events and behaviour. One in five women in a UK survey said they would like to have their bridesmaids sign a contract that contained provisions governing things like weight gain, 'intentional' pregnancy (tear in the condom is apparently okay) and hairstyle. For examples and stories, just Google 'bridesmaid contract'. The contract that pops up most often may or may not be a piss-take—the insanity of the wedding world makes it impossible to tell. One US bride emailed a contract like this to her bridesmaids, allegedly as a prank, and after successive email forwarding and a viral spread on the internet she ended up on national television having to explain herself. Nonetheless, there are many reports of such contracts being used in earnest.

before she wants you tucked, sucked, preened and undergoing all sorts of metrosexual manscaping. But let's give such brides the benefit of the doubt and let them cop to temporary insanity.

In such cases, it may be your regretful duty to bring your bride down to earth and ever so gently let her know that insisting on weight loss, cosmetic surgery or the postponement of reproduction is both impolite and an interference with evolutionary forces. 'No matter what they do,' you might add, 'they're going to pale next to you anyway.' Yes, it's a cheap line, but when you're dealing with a crazy lady flattery is like your Kevlar. Besides, where would we men be if not for cheap lines?

OTHER STUFF: BRIDESNANNIES

One wedding book suggests that a potential bridesmaid duty is supervising the children in the wedding party. I suppose someone has to keep an eye out for the kiddies, but laying that on the bridesmaids is a little old-fashioned. These days, women read, vote, have jobs and everything. Some of them don't even cook. Children in the wedding party should be watched over at the ceremony by a combination of their parents and whoever is most familiar with them in the wedding party (as the children are more likely to respond to them). At the reception it's on the parents again but, as the little scamps run about, all the adults tend to keep an eye on them. If you really want someone *assigned* to look after the kids, then you have to arrange for paid carers. After all, if the bridesmaids are looking after the children, who's minding your groomsmen?

12

THE FOLKS

'Parents Just Don't Understand'

'God made them male and female. For this cause shall a man leave his father and mother, and cleave to his wife'
(Mark 10:6–7).

'Parents just don't understand' (The Fresh Prince).

. . . Sometimes the Bible says it best,
sometimes it's the Fresh Prince.

RE-FRESH

Before *Men in Black* and *Independence Day*, Will Smith was a streetwise rapper called the Fresh Prince telling suburban Caucasian youth how it is. His seminal anthem was 'Parents Just Don't Understand'. Too true, Mr Smith, too true.

I can't tell you how often I hear the following from recently engaged couples: 'I've already had the first fight with my mother/ father.' If you're having difficulties with your parents or your bride's parents, you're not alone. In fact, I would say it's the norm. When dealing with your parents, it's always important to be respectful, polite, loving, grateful, tactful, and so on. The last thing you or your bride should do is regress and throw a tanty, which happens with surprising frequency. That just reinforces the old parent–child dynamic, whereas this is the time to establish a break from your parents. You have to stand up for yourself and your bride in a mature manner, and the two of you need to present a united front. When you reach a real impasse you need to say, simply and calmly, that this is your marriage and your wedding and this is how it's going to be. That's much more powerful and effective than tears, shouting and drama.

STANDING TALL

There's a moment in every man's teen years when he first says 'No' to his father. Even if you're steel on the outside, you're shaking on the inside. You may have to muster that selfsame courage for your wedding. At different times you may have to say 'No' to your parents as well as your bride's parents (if she finds it difficult). You don't want your wife looking back on her wedding day with regret, so don't let *anyone* piss in her champagne. This isn't just about claiming your wedding—it's about claiming your marriage. Getting married means that you owe your first loyalty to your wife, and she to you. That can be difficult for parents to accept, and their attempts to control your wedding may be a reflection of that (I know—that's deep).

While it's important to understand where they're coming from, it's just as important to stand up for yourselves, respectfully but firmly. It was the same for your parents and their parents before them, and it will be true for your children one day: 'For everything there is a season', 'The Cat's in the Cradle', 'Footloose', and all that other coming-of-age stuff. Be polite and respectful, but don't let yourselves be bullied, guilted or pressured into anything that makes you uncomfortable. If you don't cut off the parental interference now, it will continue through to your marriage and the raising of your children.

Yo' Parents, Yo' Problem

Most parental headaches naturally come from the bride's parents, because they're usually more involved with the wedding planning. Your parents probably accept that they'll take a back seat, because that's how it was in their day. They may have a few people they would like to invite, or there may be some family tradition that would be nice for you to incorporate. Try to accommodate their reasonable requests. On the other hand, if they insist that you have a formal evening wedding or that you get married in a church, or make other demands that would seriously change the nature of the day, the absolute rule is that *your parents are your problem.*

It's neither fair nor wise to leave this to your partner. First, they're *your* parents. Second, it's not very manly to hide behind your bride's skirt when it comes to Mummy and Daddy. Third, if you piss off your parents they still have to love you (that's the rule), but that doesn't necessarily apply to your bride. Finally, you want your wife and your parents to have a good relationship. A little pain now is much better than a lifetime of dealing with strained relations among relations. In particular, you must always step in between your bride and your mother throughout your life. If in doubt, you're going to have to side with your partner (this goes double for the wedding).

Lastly, if you have to deliver the hard word to your parents, never lay the blame on your partner ('Well, the thing is, Katie doesn't really want to have kids at the reception') or her parents ('Katie's parents want to keep the numbers down, so you can't invite your work friends'). Whatever disagreements you and your bride have between yourselves, once a decision is made you have to present a united front. So be a man and take responsibility for the decision. That's what good husbands do.

TALKIN' 'BOUT *THEIR* GENERATION

Generational shifts can lead to misunderstandings between engaged couples and their parents, and they can cut in several ways. For example, it may have been the 'done thing' in your parents' day to invite their parents' work colleagues to the reception. They may expect you to do the same, even though you and your bride want a more intimate wedding. Alternatively, your mum may be shocked that you're asking for cash as a wedding gift, or your bride's father may object to a daytime wedding as too 'informal'.

Be conscious of these differences, particularly the fact that the more extravagant weddings of today were not always the norm (contrary to mythologising by the wedding industry). Your parents may have had a simple 'punch and pie' reception, which were quite common even among people of means. The explosion in wedding expenditure is a relatively recent phenomenon among all but the very wealthy. So don't be surprised if either set of parents experience some shock over your wedding budget, particularly if you're asking them to pay for any of it. They may find it 'wasteful', 'extravagant', 'showy', 'ostentatious' and a few other words I just looked up in my thesaurus. If your parents are retired or lived on a much smaller wage than you now have, your wedding budget may seem obscene (and they may be right). Tread carefully and try not to take their bewilderment personally.

PARENTAL DISAPPROVAL

We all want our parents' blessing for the nuptials, but what if one of you falls short?

Yours don't like her

What if your parents disapprove of your partner? If she's a habitual heroin user and random valuables keep disappearing, then you might want to consider their opinion. Otherwise, you'll just have to man up and support her. Let your parents know that they have to respect your decision and respect your partner as your wife (your partner, of course, should treat them with similar respect). This doesn't guarantee a happy ending, but it allows for the possibility that your parents will grow to appreciate your bride in time. A real blow-up makes that harder. If the wedding itself doesn't bring the 'rents around, grandchildren have a way of softening hard hearts. In the meantime, work on the moves to your 'I was right' dance when your parents finally realise how wrong they were. Then hope that you *are* right because no one likes divorce, and watching a parental 'I was right' dance is downright painful.

Your Money or Your Wife

> Sons and daughters whose parents refuse to be swayed have no choice but to either break their engagements or continue them without their parents' approval. Those with large fortunes at stake have traditionally found the latter to be difficult (Shaw 2001, p. 10).

It is a strong love, indeed, that baulks at the loss of a trust fund. As this is the real world and not a bad Renée Zellweger movie (is there any other kind?), such a groom might have to do something completely mad and . . . *get a damn job*. It's what the rest of us do. So, here's a big box of tissues while I play a sad, sad song on the world's smallest violin for all those grooms (and brides) who might have to give up a life of lazy luxury for the sake of the person they supposedly love.

Hers don't like you

What if your partner's parents disapprove of you? Try to understand things from their point of view. If you had a daughter that was getting married to a guy like you, what concerns would you have? If they have specific doubts (like about your financial future), try your best to address them. If they still don't approve or they just don't like you, then live to prove them wrong. Once you do, an 'I was right' dance is inadvisable. Some things that work with your parents don't fly with the in-laws.

Independent Women

Don't be surprised if your bride's parents ask you about your finances and how you're going to 'support their daughter'. This is more likely the younger you marry, particularly if it's before either of you have established careers. If you're marrying later in life (which is increasingly common), here's a classic quote from a traditional wedding book: 'Grooms who are marrying ladies long independent from their parents will probably be met by prospective in-laws with more relief than inquisitiveness' (Shaw 2001, p. 9). It's not that wedding books haven't reached the new century—they haven't quite caught up to the last one yet.

DIVORCED PARENTS

Divorced parents can be tricky, especially if they're feuding. It's particularly hard if parents are separating during the wedding process, which happened with my sister's wedding. Fortunately, both my parents acted like adults, making the situation much less difficult than it could have been. If you're not as fortunate, don't be blackmailed or bullied by squabbling parents. Explain that this is one day in their troubled relationship that they will have to act civilly to each other.

For your own part, minimise any uncomfortable or embarrassing situations for your parents (seating arrangements, photographs, toasts, and so on). You may really want photos with your whole family, including mother and father by your side, but that's asking too much if wounds are still raw.

I'll See Your Emotional Blackmail, and Raise You

In really extreme cases, one parent may refuse to come to the wedding if the other does. This is understandable in certain situations (for example, physical abuse), but if it's plain old malice that's unacceptable and the parent needs a swift kick in the arse. They have the rest of their lives to be bitter and spiteful. This is your day—one day out of their lives—when you're asking them to be civil or to at least ignore each other. If it's impossible to choose between your parents, then don't. Invite both parents, and if one refuses to come that's their call, not yours. If you want to play rough, announce that anyone who refuses to attend the wedding will be denied access to the grandchildren. It's tough but fair, and if your parents are acting like squabbling children that's how you have to treat them.

Family Feud(s)

You may have to deal with other internal family feuds, or feuds between your family and the bride's (that didn't work out so well for Romeo and Juliet, or Maria and that white guy in *West Side Story*). The rule is that the bride and groom decide who comes to the wedding and those people are to act civilly to each other or, at least, not to interact at all (you respect this by not *forcing* them to interact through seating or other arrangements). Your wedding day is not about them; it's about you.

Divorced Parents and Money

In childhood, divorce may have meant stiff competition on Christmas gifts, but your wedding is *not* a time to cultivate a competition of parental love. There may be expectations that the father is responsible for all or most of any contribution to your wedding, but there are no set rules. Your circumstances and that of your parents are what's important and tact, as always, is the watchword. If you think it's going to be prickly, avoid telling one parent the specific amount the other is giving. You could ask each parent to pay for particular aspects of the wedding, like the band, the bar, the flowers, etc. Hopefully, by avoiding exact dollar figures you can diminish potential one-upmanship or bad feelings.

DIVORCED PARENTS HORROR STORY

Rogue was getting married. Her parents, Wolverine and Mystique, had a very bitter split and didn't speak to each other, so Rogue's brother, Iceman, was the go-between during the wedding process. It got so bad that Mystique gave Iceman a cheque to give to Wolverine to pay for the cost of herself and her guests, because she didn't want her ex paying for them, but she refused to give the cheque to him directly. That's some exceptional spite, but at least they both turned up and at least Iceman dealt with most of the pain and drama for his sister's sake.

MOTHER OF THE GROOM

Mother of the groom is a difficult position. She can feel like a second fiddle to the mother of the bride, which she kind of is. Even with changing traditions, the mother of the bride is still generally more involved in the planning than your mother. You should be aware of this, because while many planning details flit in and out of your brain, your mother might care a great deal about them and you're her main source of information.

One good approach is to give your mother something specific to do. In the US, it's common for the groom's family to throw a rehearsal dinner, and that may be her project. If not, there may be one aspect of the wedding or various pre-wedding parties that she can be allocated. My mum took responsibility for a party in New York to celebrate with US friends and family who couldn't make it to the Sydney wedding. She always confirmed plans with us, but we pretty much let her run with things. It worked out great. We had a difficult task off our plate and she had a significant role to play in our wedding planning. All circumstances vary, but try

DRESSING DOWN

My mother asked me what the mother of the bride would be wearing at the wedding, but of course I had no earthly idea. I also didn't know why she was asking. Apparently, the mother of the bride has first choice on outfits and the mother of the groom should both complement her (i.e., same level of formality) without upstaging or copying her (i.e., wearing the exact same colour or designer). The idea of me describing what the mother of the bride would be wearing was laughable, even if I had some inkling, so I wisely put my bride on the phone.

A SHOWER TOO FAR

Apparently, if the couple live far from the groom's parents, the mother of the groom can throw a 'proxy shower' (Post 2006, p. 182): a shower for the bride, even when the bride can't attend. Personally, I think that's a bit silly and sounds like a gift grab. I certainly can't think of many other circumstances where a party is thrown for someone who isn't there, except for a wake (and that's a worrying comparison). It's all well and good for your mother to have something to do, but maybe you can think of something a little more useful and less made up.

to find some piece of the wedding puzzle for your mum to tackle. It will take the pressure off you to keep her informed about the heaping multitude of wedding details that you neither know nor care about.

MEET THE FOCKERS

It's good if your parents and your bride's parents can meet each other at least once before the wedding madness begins. It's much easier to be offended by an abstract set of in-laws than people you've met in the flesh. Apparently, the etiquette is for your parents to contact the bride's parents, assuming they don't already know each other well. I don't know why that is and I don't care. It just means that you may want to suggest to your parents that they invite your bride's parents for lunch, drinks, barbecue, Twister challenge or what have you.

If great distance prevents an in-person meeting, a nice letter or card followed by a phone call is a good idea. You may also want to set aside a time around the wedding when the parents (and perhaps siblings) can spend some time together without other distractions. Traditionally, a rehearsal dinner the night before the wedding served this purpose, but rehearsal dinners often blow out to include other people and your parents are too busy hosting to get quality time with your bride's parents. We had a relaxed barbecue a couple of days before the wedding just for parents and close family, which was an easy, comfortable way for the families to get to know each other a bit better.

THE DRINK-DIALLING ON HIS BUCKS' NIGHT WAS ONE THING, BUT THE DRINK-UPLOADING-to-YouTube WAS QUITE ANOTHER...

13

THE BUCKS' NIGHT

And the Hangover

'Whatever entertainment is planned,
it should not embarrass, humiliate, or endanger
the honoree or any of the guests'
(Post 2006, p. 184).

... And yet, most men would say that's
the whole bloody point.

THE FIRST RULE
OF BUCKS' NIGHT
IS . . . YOU DO NOT
TALK ABOUT BUCKS'
NIGHT.

THE SECOND RULE
OF BUCKS' NIGHT
IS . . . YOU *DO NOT*
TALK ABOUT BUCKS'
NIGHT.

The 1999 surreal pugilist film *Fight Club*, starring Brad Pitt and Edward Norton, laid down the Fight Club rules. A number of the Fight Club rules are also applicable to bucks' night, but most important are the first two (noted on the previous page).

FIGHT CLUB RULES

One of the first things to learn about good, open communication is knowing when *not* to communicate. Stuff is going to go down at your bucks' night. You may think your bride is cool with it, because she accepts that boys will be boys and everybody knows what goes on at a bucks' night, but you never know how she'll react. There's a difference between the abstract idea of strippers and a particular stripper, with a particular pair of breasts, being rubbed in the face of her particular husband-to-be while sitting in his particular lap.

She really didn't need to know, didn't want to know and, after learning about it, wished she didn't know. This doesn't give you carte blanche to lie endlessly to your wife (or to cheat and cover up, because you *will* get caught). Bucks' nights fall into a special category, recognised by both sides, where white lies of omission are best for all concerned. It's a 'don't ask, don't tell' policy, or what former US defence secretary Donald Rumsfeld called 'known unknowns', as your partner generally knows what you're omitting.

It's not just your bride that you have to consider— remember that women talk. One groom made the mistake of spilling the beans to his bride about his bucks' night. As it turned out, she didn't mind the extracurriculars. So, no harm done, right? Wrong, because she talked to the partners of the other boys at the bucks' night about what they'd been up to, and one of the WAGs got very upset. If you or any of your bucks' night co-conspirators spill to any of your partners, *all* of the partners are likely to hear about it and at least one of them is bound to be upset. That's why the bucks' night rules apply to everyone, including *you*.

Other Fight Club Rules

Several of the other Fight Club rules also relate to bucks' night.

The third rule is, if the buck yells 'Stop!', goes limp, taps out, the night is over. Every man has his limit, and once the buck reaches his it's time to pack it in. You don't force tequila down the throat of a comatose buck and you don't do anything *too* horrible to his body.

The sixth rule—no shirt, no shoes—sometimes applies. It depends on what kind of night's been planned.

The seventh rule always applies: bucks' night will go on as long as it has to. Make sure none of the revellers have any important plans the next morning (a Friday or Saturday night is *highly* recommended). Everyone should carry on until the buck taps out, in accordance with rule three. This is the symbolic end of his bachelor freedom, so bailing on the buck is not an option.

OTHER RULES

And the Fight Club rules are just the beginning.

'Never, Never Leave Your Wingman'

If there's one thing we learned from *Top Gun*, it's to always watch the canopy when you're ejecting from an F-14 in a flat spin (sorry, Goose). That said, the crucial *Top Gun* rule of engagement for bucks' night is: 'You never, never leave your wingman.' (Spoken by Jester, this line is directly preceded by one of the most contradictory lines in movie history: 'That was some of the best flying I've seen yet—right up to the part where you got killed.') This especially applies to the best man. If some of the boys want to kick on after the buck heads for the hard deck and calls 'no joy', that's fine, but that doesn't mean dumping the buck in a cab and throwing the driver a fifty. It means flying Cougar all the way back to base. (On an unrelated note, be sure to check out the Coors Light 'mighty wingman' ad on YouTube.)

Never the Night Before, Dumbarse

I don't care if your bucks' is being held at an AA meeting or if the best man has planned a day of picking posies—YOU NEVER HAVE YOUR BUCKS' PARTY THE DAY BEFORE THE WEDDING, NEVER EVER.

The logic that 'well, it's an evening wedding, and I'll be over my hangover by then' is stupid and wrong. The sole purpose of your crew will be to get you drunker than you've been in your life. On the first night of my bucks' weekend, I had to throw a shot glass across the balcony to keep one friend from screaming at me to do more shots. The next day we went for an ocean swim and I soon realised that I wasn't hung-over . . . I was still drunk.

At the barest, barest minimum you need to have the bucks' party two days before the wedding, and that's if you don't have a rehearsal dinner or similar function to attend the next day. Really, you want to do it weeks or months before the wedding. Give yourself and your mates some time to recover, and make bail, if necessary. If having your bucks' well ahead of the wedding means you can't have everyone there, then so be it. It's more important to have a bride on your wedding day than your old rugby buddy at your bucks'.

Do Not Meet Up

Ideally, your bucks' will be on the same day that your partner is having her hens'. That way she'll be too busy with her own debauchery to worry about yours, and vice versa. However, *it is an extraordinarily bad idea to meet up with your bride and her friends later in the evening.* I cannot for the life of me understand why anyone would do this, yet I've heard a number of disaster stories.

First off, it's likely that both you and your bride are going to be very drunk, and not everyone makes a good drunk. You could easily get into a fight in that condition or one

CRASHING

If your bride isn't spending the night elsewhere on your bucks' night, your best move is to crash with your best man or another groomsmen so that she doesn't see, hear or smell you when you get home. Worse yet, if she's been on her hens' you two may cuddle up for a drunk hump and, no matter what we tell our children, *that's* where babies come from. This buffer also gives your best man a chance to get some greasy food in you, clean you up and flush out that hangover the next day, before you front up to your blushing bride.

of you could be disgusted with the other's condition (you will probably be the disgusting one). Also, this is the most likely time for bucks' night rules one and two to be broken because, as the Latins say, *in vino veritas* (in wine there is truth). You and your mates are on the piss and just back from some den of iniquity. Judgement is impaired and tongues are looser. Avoid this high-risk situation by staying away from your bride, and all other women of your acquaintance, on your bucks' night, and the same should apply to all your merry (and married) men.

Transportation

Don't be cheap or stupid. Arrange for a hire car or get taxis or a minibus on your bucks' night. A designated driver is unrealistic, unless he's a true teetotaller. Even then, it's unfair asking him to drive a bunch of drunks home at dawn. So, whatever it costs, make sure you use sober, hired drivers for the evening, get a hotel room in the city or do whatever it takes to make sure that none of your boys gets behind a wheel that night.

No Photos, Please

There should be a prohibition against pictures and video (or audio) recording of any sort at the bucks' night, at least after things start getting crazy. A picture says a thousand words, so this is really a corollary of the two core bucks' night rules.

ONLY IN THE MOVIES

In *The Hangover*, after photos of the bucks' night are discovered the men agree to view them *once* and then delete them forever. That's just the movies. It's much safer if photos never existed.

Your humiliation is not meant to extend beyond your small circle of mates. It's only a matter of time before we see a story about a wedding called off because some moronic grooms- man posted bucks' night photos on Facebook, seen by the bride, her family, the groom's boss and anyone else travers- ing the World Wide Web. Your partner might forgive your drunken shenanigans. She will *not* forgive you for humiliating her in front of her friends, family and co-workers. The only record of your night should be your foggy, blurred, booze- streaked memory. As with other bucks' night rules, this is for the protection of your fellow revellers as well as yourself.

BOUNDARIES

> Hi, come on in! Drugs to the right, hookers to the left (Brad, *The Bachelor Party*).

There's a certain amount of friendly sadism that occurs during bucks' nights and, as with any S&M relationship, it's important to have a 'safe word'. Which is to say, you need to set some boundaries. Talk to your best man about any ground rules that you want to set. If you think a well-mean- ing groomsman will arrange a hooker and that's just not your bag (any more), then make that clear. The more puritanical among you may even be offended by strippers. Fair enough, but your friends may not have the same . . . um . . . aversion, so you should let them know.

Where's the Line, Anyway?

Different people have different lines (more importantly, different *women* have different lines). I would say that most women (though not all) accept that porn and strippers are constituent parts of a bucks' night. If you already let slip about times you've been to strip clubs, you may have some sense of your partner's feelings on the subject. Even if your bride's okay with it in general, assume that she does not want to know details. One good thing about your best man doing the planning is it gives you *plausible deniability*.

SILLY GEESE

During the 2007 campaign, the story broke that Kevin Rudd had paid a visit to Score's strip club in New York years before. Rudd said that he told his wife he'd been a 'silly goose'. It just shows how great a spin artist the Ruddster is. What wife could be worried about the indiscretions of a man who'd refer to himself as a 'silly goose'?

Regardless, few brides are going to accept their groom sleeping with a prostitute, because forking over cash doesn't change the fact that you're having sex with another woman shortly before your wedding . . . which kind of kills the romance.

To determine your bucks' night limits, *assume*, despite all precautions, that your partner finds out about what you did. If she's going to be annoyed, angry, piqued, irritated, disappointed, unnerved, send you to confession or put you on the couch for a spell, then you had a good time and mostly got away with it. If she's going to fly into a rage, cry herself to sleep for weeks, get her brothers to break your legs or call off the wedding, then you've crossed the line. Have a great time, but don't let one night spoil your life or that of the woman you love.

VEGAS EXPECTATIONS

One bride whose groom went to Las Vegas for his bucks' was shocked to discover that her husband-to-be spent the night around mostly naked women (i.e., strippers). Frankly, if the groom is having his bucks' night in Vegas, the bride should be damn glad he didn't wake up in jail with a heroin addiction, handcuffed to a male hooker.

ADVICE

Here are a few more bits of fatherly advice.

I Want a New Drug

I've always been confused about how people get caught with drugs. I read about a girl who died at a concert because she swallowed three hits when she spotted the sniffer dogs coming her way. If you want one last hurrah with narcotics I'm not going to be your public service message, but don't get caught or dead. I've never heard of cops going around busting down doors of homes to arrest people for personal use. So, if you must, then do it at home and *leave it there*. Don't take it out to dinner, clubbing, bar-hopping, concerts, or anywhere else that could get you thrown in jail so close to your wedding.

For the love of God, don't bring drugs on a plane or into a foreign country. You'd be too stupid to live, and some countries will make that point by executing you. For the same reason, don't buy illegal drugs in a foreign country (hey, there's always Amsterdam). You're getting married, and while that doesn't mean trading in your hash pipe for a pocket watch, it does mean taking some responsibility for yourself like avoiding stupid and unnecessary risks.

BUCKS' PARTY MOVIES (NO, NOT THAT KIND)

For a chilling, cautionary tale about drug use on a bucks' night be sure to see *The Hangover*. Actually, I've just checked the box-office receipts and DVD sales, and you already have . . . twice. For another cinematic exploration of the bucks' night gone wrong have a look at *The Bachelor Party*, an eighties throwback featuring a fresh-faced Tom Hanks. I'll see your tiger in the bathroom and raise you a cocaine-snorting donkey.

It's a Marathon, Not a Sprint

You have a whole night or weekend of entertainment planned for you, and it would be a shame to miss any of it. There's the temptation to go hard out of the gates, but try to pace yourself. You want to experience it all (and remember some of it). You don't want your friends dragging you around town like *Weekend at Bernie's* while they have all the fun. On my bucks' weekend, I drank so much on Friday night that I did myself in for Saturday. Some of my mates couldn't make it up until Saturday and were a bit disappointed that I could only force down a few beers on the second night.

Don't Be Stupid

This is a general admonition to cover a multitude of sins (well, sins are inevitable—make that acts of historic stupidity). So, don't get drunk before or during rock climbing. Don't drunk-dial or text your bride, or tweet anything during the proceedings. In fact, hand over your mobile to your best man at the beginning of the night and instruct him to keep you away from any form of communication device. Don't get a lap dance from the stripper with the exceptionally large Adam's apple. Don't run with scissors or other sharp implements. Don't get bogged down in a protracted Middle East engagement with Islamic extremists who are incited by your very presence. You get the idea.

Father Knows Best (But Sees Little)

If you want to include the older generation in your bucks' night but don't want your father, and especially not your father-*in-law*, to join in the less seemly points of the evening, consider dividing your bucks' into stages. You can start with a nice dinner at a good steakhouse—which includes fathers, uncles and so on—and then the young bucks can move on to the age-inappropriate activities.

BROTHER BEWARE

Just days before his wedding, the Flash and his Justice League mates ran down to a nearby party town for the bucks' night. It happened that the bride's brother went to university in this same town, but he missed out on the invite. The Flash came back the next day, a little worse for wear for the formal rehearsal dinner, to find neither his bride nor any of her family speaking to him because of the slight to the bride's brother. Not a good spot to be in the day before the wedding (I suppose he could have made a run for it).

IDEAS AND ALTERNATIVES

> Let's have a bachelor party with chicks and guns and fire
> trucks and hookers and drugs and booze! (Rudy, *The
> Bachelor Party*).

The planning should really be up to your best man and
the groomsmen, but it's sensible to point them in the right
direction and they may ask for your views on this or that.
The main thing is that the plans reflect you. If you're a big
sailor, then a day on a boat won't steer you wrong. A camping
trip works great for hiking enthusiasts. And so on.

If your friends are stuck for ideas there's no limit to the
possibilities, plenty of which are out there on the web (just
enter 'bucks' night' in your favourite search engine . . . okay,
Google). Certain companies specialise in organising bucks'
nights and trips. Some of it is pretty predictable, like dinner
and strip-club tours for X dollars per head, but I'm not
judging. If you poke around (no pun intended), you can find
some interesting alternatives. Below are a few different types
of activities that your mates might consider.

Big Night Out

This is your classic bucks' night. You hit the town big, paint it
red and stay out till dawn. There're all sorts of variations. You
can start at a restaurant that serves up a whole roast suckling
pig. You can plan a specific pub crawl. You can have a theme
(cricket, Mexican, or Gilbert and Sullivan musicals . . . just
kidding). The buck can (and should) be made to dress like
an idiot. The buck and other revellers can be given different challenges (e.g., first man to get a girl's phone number

makes the rest do a shot of his choosing). The possibilities go on and on.

Big Night In

You could have your big night at a friend's place, a hotel room or some other static location (try to avoid using your place—clean-up's a bitch). Hanging out with your mates, watching porn and getting stupid is great fun, but it's best to frame things around some activity like a poker night. On the web you'll find companies who will organise a poker night for you, at your place or theirs, that can include scantily clad (or non-clad) waitresses and dealers. In fact, a little internet research proved that you could have scantily clad women added to almost any bucks' activity: sailing, fishing, poker, bobsledding and so on.

Bucks' Weekend

Why limit yourself to just one night of moral turpitude? The bucks' weekend is becoming increasingly popular and, again, the possibilities are endless. You can have a golf weekend, sail around the Whitsundays, go camping, hiking or canyoning, do a wine tour or visit some breweries. It's just a matter of what you and your mates enjoy. For my bucks' we rented a house by the beach, got drunk, ate meat, played poker, watched sophomoric movies (*Harold & Kumar*, *Caddyshack*) and staggered down to the beach occasionally for a sobering swim. It may have been the best weekend of my life (sorry, baby). We liked it so much that the same crew got together and did it again less than a year later.

Big Trip

An extension of the bucks' weekend is the bucks' big trip, including foreign locales. This takes things to another level, but if you and your friends have the scratch and the time then go for your life. These bucks' trips became particularly popular in the UK, with their almighty pound and cheap flights across Europe, but that may have changed in the wake of the global financial crisis. The brothels and brownie joints of Amsterdam must really be hurtin'.

Wussified Options

If you want an alternative to the traditional booze-guzzling, strip-club, Dad-bailing-you-out-of-jail bucks' party, then do any of the things noted above (e.g., steak dinner, golf weekend, poker night) or anything else you like to do without the drugs, booze, strippers and jail time. There's no shame in not doing the traditional stripper event. Like Homer Simpson, I too 'enjoy a snifter of port around the holidays' and I once occasioned establishments where excessive heat required the women to remove their clothes. Still, at a certain point in a man's life, frequenting strip clubs just becomes sad—and if the DJ knows your name, it's time to seek help.

PLANNING

Here are a few things to consider when planning your night of nights.

Budget

Generally speaking, your groomsmen should take care of you for the evening (for a weekend away you should insist on paying your share of flights, accommodation, etc., but the boys can certainly shout you dinner, drinks and amenities if they offer). However, consider who you want to participate in the bucks'. Not everyone has equal finances and, particularly in darker economic times, one or more of your mates may not be able to front up for a weekend trip or an exorbitant night on the town. Set a budget with your best man that will work for everyone (within reason) and let him work within those parameters.

Big Buck Hunter

Some finer establishments (nice restaurants, wanky pubs, casinos) might not allow bucks' parties, so you could find yourselves barred at the door or arsed out. In their opinion, bucks' parties can be more trouble than they're worth. Make sure your best man looks into this as he makes the plans, particularly for any key parts of the night. Also, don't try to get cute and pretend you're something else. A bucks' party crew is obvious from a mile away. You can rage against this discrimination if you like, but even if your drunk lawyer friend spouts off about your constitutional rights to drink and be merry, by the time the case makes it to the High Court your kids will be off to work.

Supply List

There are some things you may want to take with you for your bucks' party as a precautionary measure:

1. Taxi numbers are a must, if you don't have a hire car, limo, party bus, etc.

2. Emergency cash stash (lap dance is not an emergency—but it's close). If you wake up in a gutter, hidden cash can be your ticket home.
3. Passport and visa for overseas trips and driver's licence or some other identification for local excursions.
4. Map of area hospitals and emergency telephone numbers (especially poison control).
5. Just for good measure: riot gear, handcuffs (and *keys* to the handcuffs), snake-bite kit and portable defibrillator.

The flip side of this is things you *should not* bring, like: drugs, your phone, any photographic or audiovisual recording device, or a sense of shame.

14

THE TOAST

Brevity is the Soul of Wit

*'According to most studies, people's number one fear is
public speaking. Number two is death . . . This means, to
the average person, if you go to a funeral, you're better off
in the casket than doing the eulogy'*
(Jerry Seinfeld).

. . . My number one fear is having to sit through
the *Sex and the City* movie again.

If a speaker is funny, clever and good with a turn of phrase and he knows it, there are no problems. If a speaker is not particularly funny and breaks into a soaking sweat in front of a crowd that's fine too, as long as he knows it. The real danger is if a person thinks he's funny and he's just not. So, before you or your best man tries to give people an hour of Robin Williams stand-up, you need to check with a trusted friend and ask, flat out, if you're as funny as you think you are. No one's looking for Barack Obama in a wedding toast, just sincerity, brevity and a bit of levity.

This chapter provides guidance that applies to any and all toasts, but particularly for you and your best man (you can loan him the book or, better yet, buy him his own copy).

SCARED TO DEATH (AND BEYOND)

On most fear surveys, public speaking tops death as the number-one cause of knee-clattering and pants-pissing. However, in a 2008 Newspoll survey of Australians, death managed to edge out a public spray as the top Aussie fear . . . but only just. Chalk that up to an Australian love for public spectacle, or the particularly gruesome list of ways you might pass over Down Under (spider, snake, jellyfish, shark, or having a go at Barry Hall).

The Best Man's Pocket Guide provides the following advice on dealing with your crippling fear (or constipation—you be the judge): 'Contract your stomach muscles as tight as you can and then relax them. Clench your hands into fists as tight as you can . . . and then relax . . . Push your arms tightly into your side and then relax. Lastly, press your feet firmly into the floor and then relax them' (Bryant 2005, p. 182). Even if this succeeds in relaxing you, by that time everyone in the audience will either think you're a complete nutter or that you have to go potty.

To calm your nerves, remember that guests at a wedding want you to do well, want to laugh and be happy, and they're probably half-drunk. It's one of the easiest crowds to please, and there's little chance of hecklers (though it's been known to happen).

DON'T BE GENERIC

If you can't speak well or write a good speech, there's a great temptation to use a generic toast from a wedding book, speech book or website. *Please don't do this.* I have spent many painful hours trawling through these generic speeches and they're crotch-kickingly awful. More importantly, using a generic toast says very little about your relationship with the person you're toasting. Your remarks don't have to be Shakespeare or Oscar Wilde. It doesn't even have to be that good, but it does have to be *personal and genuine.*

If you're really stuck, a generic toast can be an okay place to start. It will hit the major points and have a basic structure, with a beginning, middle and end. What you need to do then is get inside it. If you wouldn't describe marriage as the 'greatest adventure', then don't. Change the parts that don't sound like you. Then make sure to add in personal details about the people you're toasting and your relationship with them. Sometimes, by working within someone else's words, your ideas start to flow and you end up with something very much your own.

Beware of Generic Platitudes

While they were once a nice turn of phrase, overuse has made generic platitudes stale and lifeless. They may be hard to avoid completely, but use them sparingly. A speech weighed down by them will be flat and impersonal. Here are a few examples of stale sayings expressed in fresher language:

1. 'When I think of people that should be together, I immediately think of Mike and Sara' (Bryant 2005, p. 141). This is a great sentiment for any toast to the bride and groom but the specific expression is so clichéd, as are the tired phrases 'meant for each other' and 'belong together'. Instead, consider the following: 'Watching how Mike and Sara are together, I have never known any two people who belong to each other so completely.' That's the same sentiment and some of the same words, but the slight changes make the expression of it new and fresh.

2. 'From the bottom of my heart . . . may your love survive the test of time, and last forever' (Bryant 2005, p. 150). That's a triple generic platitude, the last of which is redundant. As an alternative, try: 'I have great faith that your love will see you through the difficult times and bring both of you the greatest happiness in all your days together.'

3. Instead of 'special day' or 'joyous occasion', try 'singular moment' or 'blissful time'. For example, 'We are gathered here on this special day . . .' becomes 'As friends and family, we draw together in this singular moment . . .'

Individually, these changes seem subtle, but they make an amazing difference when carried through an entire speech. It's like giving an old pair of shoes a new shine. My specific changes should work until this book becomes so popular that the changes evolve into generic platitudes too. The point is, you can easily do what I've done with a thesaurus, a little patience and someone to listen to your drafts.

Old Lines and Bad Jokes

'There is a saying that the old lines are the best, and they are not wrong' (Love 2007, p. 92). No, they are most *definitely* wrong.

You know the problem with old lines? They're old. And few of them were funny the first time around. People just smile and nod out of politeness, and by the time you use an old line people may be tired of smiling and nodding. I have heard suggested lines that would make a coma patient cringe: 'It's OK to have sixteen wives: four better, four worse, four richer and four poorer' (Love 2007, p. 92). Is that funny? No, it's not. It's not funny in a groaning, 'how lame was that' way. It's not funny in the way a movie can be so bad that it's actually funny (like the 1995 film *Showgirls*). It's not funny in any way whatsoever.

Definitely avoid the whole 'marriage sucks and wives are terrible shrews' line of jokes, which seem particularly popular in Britain. For example: 'Never forget the five rings of marriage: Engagement RING, Wedding RING, SuffeRING, TortuRING and EnduRING' (Bryant 2005, p. 152). The quip manages to be both lame and misogynistic.

Don't confuse humour with jokes. Jokes are forced, contrived, stale and rarely funny in a speech. Humour injects life into your speech, keeps people interested and balances the inherent sentimentalism of a wedding toast. It's creative and specific to the people you're toasting—their personality, quirks and circumstances. Self-deprecating humour is always good, like the following example for a groom: 'I would like to thank my best man, Tom, for inspiring me to leave my lucrative career in banking to become a writer. Which reminds me, Tom, the bride's father would like to have a quick word with you in the corner.'

FAKE QUESTION, REAL ANSWER

Q: Do you feel bad telling people who gave generic wedding speeches that their toasts were lame?

A: No. It's too late to help those people. I try to focus on all the people I can *save* from giving lame wedding toasts.

Quotations

If you need some perfect pearl of wit or wisdom to polish up your toast and can't muster it yourself, a quotation or line from a poem is a fine way to go. Just don't make it too sappy or generic. If you've heard the quote in a movie or at another wedding or celebration, it means it's been used a lot. Pick something else. There are many quotation sites on the internet and books of quotations at your local library, often organised by topic area. For your toast it's even better if the quote has some connection to you as a couple, like your bride's favourite poet or a line from a song you heard on your first date (as long as it isn't 'I Touch Myself' by the Divinyls).

TELL A STORY

Stories are more personal than generic lines, more poignant than platitudes and much funnier than jokes. The poets and songwriters have used all the good lines. So, tell a story that demonstrates *why* you love your bride or what it is that you love about her. Is she unusually kind, sympathetic, courageous, generous, funny or self-sacrificing? If so, don't just say that when there's a story that illustrates it.

The following is a very simple guide for the wedding speech-writing process:

1. Focus on a particular quality or several qualities of the person you want to toast.
2. Think of a story or anecdote that demonstrates that quality.
3. Tell that story.

The following are two different groom toasts to the same bride and maid of honour, the first of which relies on description while the second tells a story.

Description Version

Lisa is such a caring, unselfish person, who is very devoted to her family, especially her sister, Anna. That devotion is one of the reasons I fell in love with Lisa. That's why it's so special that all of Lisa's family can be here to celebrate with us today, especially Anna.

Story Version

> I remember when Lisa's sister, Anna, got sick. Lisa dropped everything—her work, a holiday we had planned—and went immediately to Anna's side to help care for her. It was a difficult time for everyone, and it was a significant time for me. When I saw the way Lisa cared for her family I realised how much I wanted to be a part of her family, and her life, for the rest of mine. So, it means very much to both Lisa and me that Anna could be by our side today, to witness the love that she helped inspire.

The first toast is nice, but the second is much more affecting. Notice that nowhere in the second version does the groom spell out Lisa's qualities, describe the relationship between the sisters or say directly that he loves her. All those things are communicated more powerfully through the story. The audience doesn't just know the groom loves Lisa, they understand the nature of that love.

Lastly, resist the urge to spell out how the story exemplifies the person's quality (i.e., don't say, 'Wasn't that a nice story, showing just how unselfish Mike is?', as suggested in *The Best Man's Pocket Guide*, Bryant 2005, p. 139). The story should speak for itself, and that kind of statement is distracting and insults your audience.

Story for the Best Man

Just for good measure, here's an example of a story-based best man toast to the couple:

> I got a call from Matt one day, who could barely contain his excitement. I asked him what all the fuss was about. Was

the new Jimmy Choo line out? 'Very funny,' he said. Apparently, Belinda just passed a major professional exam, and she was so relieved and Matt was so proud of her. An hour after putting down the phone with Matt, I got a call from Belinda. She was excited too, and I thought I knew why. Before I could congratulate her on the exam, she blurted out that Matt just got this important promotion and she was over the moon. Neither Matt nor Belinda found time to tell me about their own success that day. Each was too wrapped up in the happiness of the other, and I think that tells you all you need to know about Matt and Belinda and their love for each other. So, my toast for Matt today is to all the happiness for Belinda, and my toast for Belinda is to all the happiness for Matt. To the happy couple.

Advanced Story Telling

1. *Transitions.* My brother's best-man toast for me featured a masterful transition from a humorous story from our childhood to a poignant example of when I was there for him in our adulthood. The best toasts will have transitions that reflect the transformation that the wedding represents. Stories of change from childhood to adulthood or from bachelorhood to devoted partner are good examples. There are transitions of tone too, from humour to sentiment. You don't need to *force* transitions into your speech. They develop naturally from the stories you tell, but being conscious of them as you write helps make the speech stronger.

2. *Time shifts.* Time periods are always good for a laugh, and provide a natural transition mechanism (yesterday to today). The clothing and hairstyles of the seventies, the films and TV shows of the eighties or the music of the nineties help set the scene to embarrass your toasting subject in a fairly harmless way.

THEMES

The following are some suggested themes for different types of toasts.

Themes for the Bride

Here are some qualities/themes to think about when toasting your bride:

1. Her relationship with her family and caring nature, as per the Lisa example. This kills a few birds with one stone, as you may also be able to compliment her parents and family.

2. Explain how she has made you 'a better man'.

3. The moment you knew you loved her or wanted to marry her (and why).

4. Stories of good works or deeds, especially those that are not well known.

5. Stories of great courage or self-sacrifice.

> **JACK**
>
> In *As Good as it Gets*, Jack Nicholson's obsessive-compulsive curmudgeon melts Helen Hunt's heart with the line 'you make me want to be a better man' (it helps if you imagine Nicholson's voice and arched eyebrows).

For an injection of humour, self-deprecation is often safer than tackling the bride. Stories about your ineptitudes in wooing her are always good toasting fodder.

Themes for the Groom and the Couple

The best man speech is like a eulogy for two people who are still alive. You're talking about where they've been, who they are and the people they've become together. Here are some themes for the best man to think about when toasting the groom or couple:

1. The conversion of the confirmed bachelor (wasn't going to get married until 50, if ever).
2. Changes in the groom since he met his bride, both humorous and positive.
3. Any sickening story of how cutesy-wutesy the groom became once he fell in love.
4. Changes from boyhood to manhood (especially for a brother or childhood friend).

It's not a bad idea for the best man to get some guidelines from you and the bride on the tenor of the toast, as you're going to have a much better idea about the audience. He should also check with you about any subjects or stories that are off limits.

WARNINGS

There are a few things to watch out for when planning any wedding toast.

Length

Toasts are a bit of an art form in Australia, so they tend to be longer here. In speaking terms a few minutes can be a *very long time*, so nothing should be much longer than that. The number of toasts is also a factor. If there are going to be a few then you'll probably only want one 'keynote' toast, traditionally done by the best man, and the other speakers should be briefer (e.g., the father of the bride welcoming the guests). You don't want toasts going on for 25 to 30 minutes—that's testing your guests' attention span. If you and the families are big talkers, then split the toasts into two sessions to give your guests a break. At one wedding I went to, my bladder was ready to explode by the time the succession of interminable toasts ended. I wasn't alone—there was a rush to the toilets as soon as the last speaker put the mic down.

Timing is Everything

Back in my single days, my ability to talk to women while drinking roughly correlated to my pool game. After a few drinks I loosened up, stopped thinking too much and the balls found the pockets like water down a drain. After a few *more* drinks, I started seeing three balls for every one actually on the table before eventually performing samurai moves with my cue. The same goes for the toasts. Time them when both the toasters and the audience have had enough social lubrication to find that happy place, but not so much to put them in the *bad* place. You don't want the best man slurring through his remarks or your father saying what he *really* thinks of your mother's new partner. Many pool games, pick-up opportunities and wedding receptions have been lost this way.

DYING AT A WEDDING

After a charmingly befuddled Hugh Grant (Charles) delivers a top best man speech in *Four Weddings and a Funeral*, his foppish friend, Tom, follows with this flop: 'When Bernard told me he was getting engaged to Lydia, I congratulated him because all his other girlfriends were such complete dogs. Although, may I say how delighted we are to have so many of them here today. I'm particularly delighted to see Camilla, who many of you will remember as the first person Bernard asked to marry him. If I remember rightly, she told him to sod off . . . And lucky for Lydia that she did.' Interestingly, there are only subtle differences between the two toasts, but they lead to very dissimilar results.

Things Not to Do (Best Man)

There are some specific things for the best man to avoid:

1. Don't talk too much about yourself, being the best man, how hard it is to do the speech or the process of writing the speech. You are not the story.

2. Don't joke about being the *best* man, as in: 'I personally want to thank you . . . for finally admitting, after all these years, that I am in fact the "best man"' (Bryant 2005, p. 208). Don't joke that the groom wrote the nice parts about himself in the toast or

that he paid you to say it. Guess what? You're *not* the first guy to think of those lines. So, hold those clever quips back, introduce yourself and move on to the bride and groom.

3. Don't make fun of the stupid wedding stuff (ridiculous decorations, bridesmaid dresses, pink stretch Humvee limo) even though they're screaming for it. It will not make the bride happy and could piss off the families as well.

Crossing the Line

Taking the piss is a great Aussie tradition, and wedding toasts are a prime opportunity. The best man gets stuck into the groom, the groom has his right of reply, and a few other barbs are traded around. Of course, it's a delicate balance between *embarrassing* and *humiliating* someone. Part of this is knowing your audience. Material appropriate for the bucks' night is decidedly inappropriate for Great Aunt Liddy with the heart condition. Another part is knowing topics to avoid, like ex-girlfriends. It's mostly common sense and judgement. When in doubt ask someone else (with a sense of decorum), and if still in doubt then don't say it. Better to drop a potential laugh than risk an awkward silence. To assist you, I've provided a brief list of contrasts:

FUNNY	NOT FUNNY
Hopeless with women	Mad rooter/past relationships
Listens to Céline Dion/Indigo Girls	Slept with Céline Dion/Indigo Girls

FUNNY	NOT FUNNY
Youthful drinking incidents (within reason)	Alcoholism, drug abuse, gambling problems or any kind of addiction
Stupid behaviour	Criminal behaviour
Never picks up the bill	Indebtedness or unemployment
Clever double entendres	Cursing and vulgarity
Kiwis sleeping with sheep	Aussies sleeping with sheep
Lack of personal sporting prowess	Failure of favourite sporting team
Male/female interaction	Ethnic humour
Social politics	Religion and politics
Ridiculousness of other weddings	Ridiculousness of *this* wedding

Props and Games

A great way to liven up your speech and make it more memorable is to incorporate a game, stunt or prop into the proceedings (Bryant 2005, p. 160).

A cruelly embarrassing slideshow or video, done well (funny, not lewd), could be a great complement to a wedding toast, though longer productions are best reserved for a rehearsal dinner or similar event. Otherwise, stay away from props and *do not* turn yourself into a clown, magician or game-show host. You are not to perform tricks, pass through the audience like a lounge act or ask the bride and groom to 'pick a card'. You are not to invite the guests to write limericks about the couple, play any type of game or hold a sweepstakes for guessing the length of the speeches. In fact, you are not to ask for guest participation of any kind. I only mention these things because they've been suggested in other wedding books and they are universally lame.

Delivery

1. *First impressions.* When you step up to the mic, first impressions are important, so first off don't piss yourself. Smiling is good, but if you do it too long without saying something you'll come off like a mental patient. Keep a tall, open posture without thrusting your nipples at the audience.
2. *Eye contact.* Move your gaze around a bit and don't just stare at the hot girls. A little lingering is fair, if you're the best man, but if you're the groom avoid the hot girls altogether (except for your new wife).
3. *Voice.* Your tone should be friendly and conversational, like talking to your best friend's mum (who you wouldn't cuss in front of).

PREPARATION

The following are a few suggestions for speech preparation:

1. *Thanks all around.* There are different traditions concerning who thanks whom in the wedding toasts. What matters is that everyone (parents, groomsmen,

bridesmaids, distant travellers, etc.) gets mentioned by someone. Coordinate with the speakers to ensure that everyone is covered and that there isn't too much duplication (e.g., not everyone needs to mention the bride's grandfather, who passed away last year). For your toast, start with the list of people *you* need to mention and thank (don't forget to include your bride). It's easy to miss someone in the heat of the moment, and you *will* regret it.

2. *Write it down.* If you're an experienced speaker, you might be attempted to wing it and impress people with your fluid delivery. I wung it (or winged it—I never know which) and found myself a bit shell-shocked, stumbled a bit, and forgot to thank a very important person. So don't worry about looking like the vice-captain of your high-school debating team—have note cards. You might never need to look at them, but at least you have backup if the rush of the moment throws you for a loop. If you're less confident, then it's fine to read from a written speech. Just make sure to look up from the page to connect with your audience now and again.

3. *Practise.* Even a great speech doesn't stand a chance if poorly delivered. You might blurt the speech out in an incomprehensible rush to get through it as quickly as possible. Alternatively, you might read it from the page in a uniform monotone, like a train conductor announcing the upcoming stations. Speeches, like stories, need pauses, emphases, inflection, cadence, build-up and climax. Practise reading your speech

out loud, as if you were telling a bedtime story to a child, and you'll hear where these different elements fit. When you're ready, read it to another person for their thoughts. Practice also helps you memorise the speech, if that's your goal.

4. *Relax*? When you give your speech, the first thing you must do is *relax. Relax, goddamn it!* Sorry, but I love the insistent relaxation advice in wedding books, because it actually stresses you out about not being relaxed. This is one of my favourites: 'Try to empty your mind of all thoughts' (Bryant 2005, p. 182). I suppose it worked for George W Bush—he was never nervous when he spoke. Don't picture everyone naked either. There are too many relatives in the room, and people will wonder why you're poking out your eyes.

ORDER AND ORGANISATION

The following is a typical order of reception toasts:

1. Welcome from the father of the bride.
2. Best man (keynote speech).
3. Maid of honour.
4. Groom and/or bride.

As with many traditional things, feel free to disregard this order at your whim. There's also no requirement that all of these people give a toast. I've been to weddings where only the best man spoke. Additionally, other people might give a toast who weren't mentioned above (e.g., mother of the bride, father or mother of the groom, grandparent, etc.). As always, do what makes the most sense for you. Just be sure to know who's speaking, have a set order and make sure that the MC and the speakers all know that order. The wedding reception is not a time for unscheduled toasts, because they're unpredictable and you simply don't have the time. There are other occasions connected to the wedding when the floor can be opened to speakers, such as the rehearsal dinner, engagement parties and bucks' and hens' nights.

Master of Ceremonies (the MC)

Toast coordination is a time when your MC really shines. You decide the order of the toasts, but the MC marshals them on the day. The MC also makes announcements to move things along (when to be seated, cutting of the cake, first dance, etc.) and helps you stick to your schedule. He or she usually says a word or two about the bride and groom and briefly introduces the various toasters, without overshadowing the main speeches.

THE GREAT AUSSIE MC TRADITION

In the US, the MC is usually some cheesy, hired DJ who knows nothing about the couple. He's somewhere between the DJ at your Year 5 dance and the guy who announces the strippers at your local house of loose morals (sadly, it's probably the same guy). In Australia, a close friend or relative usually acts as MC, which is much better. Every couple has at least one member of their inner circle with a quick wit and a lack of self-awareness. The MC is often a member of the wedding party, but it's also a great way to include a good friend who didn't make it into a small wedding party.

15

THE BIG DAY
Too Fast, Too Furious

*'There are few spaces in life where purity, beauty,
and light fill the air with such exquisite refinement and
where time seems to stand still in reverence of the sacred.
Woman and man are transformed, for a moment,
into the heavenly bride and groom'*
(Paul 2000, p. 84).

. . . Hell, it's a wedding, not *Xanadu*.

XANADU

Xanadu is a paradise described in the Coleridge poem 'Kubla Khan', but it's also a 1980 film featuring Olivia Newton-John. It has one of the silliest plots and highest gag factors of any movie in history. Released at the high-water mark of disco and rollerskating, it helped to kill them both. Tragically, it was the last film of the great acting and dancing talent Gene Kelly, who knows better now.

No matter how organised you both are, and no matter how many times you pictured the day in your minds, you just can't predict how a wedding will go . . . but that's only bad if you make it so. You have a room full of 30 to 300 individuals, each with their own personalities, tastes and level of energy, all interacting with each other in a way that's hard to foresee. It's like any other party, really. It's best to adjust to the flow of the day. That doesn't mean abandoning your essential plans (first dance, cake-cutting, etc.)—it means not forcing things too much.

Once the classy jazz band finished at our wedding, I put on some modern tunes for our younger friends (mostly cheesy eighties stuff, but we can't help when we grew up). I thought everyone would get excited and storm the dance floor, but few did. I was frustrated at first, but then I looked around and saw that people weren't dancing because they were enjoying talking to each other. That was the strength of our wedding. There was great chemistry between guests, even among people who just met. Once I realised that, I relaxed, let the music go and went to enjoy everyone's company too. If I had tried to force everyone onto the dance floor with my groom authority ('this is my wedding and you must all dance now'), then I would have ruined one of the best things about our wedding—the great vibe in the room. It's all right to have an idea about how the day will go, but social events tend to find their own groove. If you go with it instead of fighting it, you're going to enjoy yourself a lot more and make better memories for you and your guests.

COLD FEET?

What if you're not sure you want to get married any more? The first thing to do is identify the reason for your change of heart. Does it have more to do with the *wedding* or the *marriage*? Are you freaking out about how much the wedding is costing, what a massive project it is or what your partner has become under the stress of it all? All those things will pass with the wedding and are manageable in the meantime (e.g., you can scale things down, help de-stress your bride and even postpone the wedding). Remember what Homer Simpson says: 'I guess some people never change. Or they quickly change and then quickly change back.' Your bride should do the latter.

I know a couple who got overwhelmed by their wedding and they did a brave thing by postponing it with an apologetic and gracious email (they got married a few months later). The wedding can be like a charging freight train

> **PARTY PLANNING**
>
> Sometimes those over-thought theme parties (Halloween, white party, pyjama) end up a flop. Then you have a random Saturday when you invite a friend over and throw a few snags on the barbecue, he brings some beer and a few other friends, the Victoria's Secret bus breaks down outside your place and you end up with one of those completely unplanned, legendary nights that people talk about for years.

and you both feel like you're tied to the tracks, but your relationship has to come first. Any real friend or loved one will understand, so don't be afraid to pull the emergency brake if that's what it takes.

If you're questioning your feelings for your bride and are no longer sure you want to spend the rest of your life with her, then you have a bigger problem. Perhaps some major event changed things, like one of you having an affair. If it's something of this order, talk to a trusted friend or family member or seek couples' counselling. Postpone the wedding, if necessary. Don't make a snap decision, but don't go forward with a marriage you're not sure about either. Just remember, *no* bloke is completely sure about *the wedding*, so don't let that be your excuse or we wouldn't have any marriages. After all, 'the world must be peopled' (*Much Ado About Nothing*, II. iii).

Lookin' for Love for All the Wrong Reasons

If you're looking for some pseudo-professional advice, an article in the *Sydney Morning Herald* ('Marriage Traps to Avoid', 4 June 2009) offers five wrong reasons for getting married from various experts to which I've supplied my own interpretation:

1. *Sexual attraction.* Well, it worked for Tom Cruise and Nicole (oh, wait). Heat between the sheets may be a necessary condition for marriage, but it's certainly not sufficient. I know for myself that going by physical attraction alone would have led to any number of bad marriage matches (sorry, Angelina).

2. *Escaping the family.* If you can't cover the rent for a place by yourself, marriage is not the solution. Try a share house and then work for that promotion (or get a job).

3. *Infatuation.* There should be a difference between the way you feel about Buffy the Vampire Slayer and the woman you're going to marry. Infatuation inevitably leads to disappointment, and occasionally to a restraining order.

4. *Ignoring signs of trouble.* If your bride just boiled your pet bunny because you glanced at another woman in the street, that's a bad sign. However, increased tension always comes with the stress of wedding planning, so try to distinguish between temporary irritability and a pattern of psychotic behaviour.

5. *Keeping your blinkers on.* We might call this the 'Lois Lane Syndrome' after the so-called *investigative* reporter who couldn't identify her tights-wearing love interest because of a lousy pair of glasses. The point is, make sure you *know* the person you're marrying before you end up with babies flying 'round the house.

PREGAME

These are just a few tips on how to deal with the final 24 hours before your wedding.

Distraction

Sitting around thinking about your wedding the day or two before it—or even the morning of—can drive you

RELAXING WITH BOND

In the opening scenes of *Licence to Kill*, a forgettable James Bond film starring the regrettable Timothy Dalton, Bond and his best CIA pal, Felix Leiter, take down a Latin American drug lord en route to Leiter's wedding, then parachute down to the church. Needless to say the bride was not pleased, but that's what happens when you make a bad Bond best man.

batty. There may not be lots to do, as most things are hopefully sorted. So, kick the footy around, go for a round of golf, hit a poker tournament or do whatever you do to relax. I went for a body bash at Bondi with my brother and some mates. Do something to take your mind off things and keep you occupied—just nothing involving too much drinking or that's likely to cause serious injury or death.

Wedding Eve

In this day and age, it's likely that your wedding night is not going to be the first physical consummation of affections between you and your not-so-blushing bride. But hey, the women are still wearing white these days, so it's always nice to pretend. One way to enhance that pretence is by sleeping separately the night before the wedding. You'll have the rest of your lives to wake up next to each other. On this last night as single people, it's nice for your bride to be with her mother, sister(s) and/or bridesmaids and for you to be with your father, brother(s) and/or groomsmen.

NO BULL

All brides are born-again virgins on their wedding night. As Annie Savoy (Susan Sarandon) assures a less-than-wholesome bride in *Bull Durham*: 'Honey, we all deserve to wear white.'

Sleeping separately also means you can both get down to business the next morning with wedding prep, which for her is an insanely complicated process. She doesn't need you distracting her. It also magnifies the moment if the first image of your bride on the wedding day is of her walking down the aisle in all her radiant glory (thanks to hours of preparation and several beauty professionals). It's far superior to her just-out-of-bed look, with hair matted to one side of her face, bad breath and lingering skin blemishes.

CASH TIP

Your bride probably isn't going to have a purse on her, so make sure you bring some cash with you to the wedding as well as ATM and credit cards. You may have forgotten about some expense (tip for your driver or coat check) and you may have some unanticipated expenses (late-night taxi, bail for your father-in-law, etc.). If you don't want to carry around a bulky wallet during the wedding, your best man can hold on to it for you (if you trust him) or just keep the few things that you need in your pocket.

Sleepless

Wedding books give varying advice on getting to sleep the night before your wedding, such as telling your bride how much you love her, writing her a love letter, or having a heart-to-heart with your father or best mates. I reckon that if you're having trouble sleeping, a warm glass of milk is the way to go. Just make sure someone, like the best man, is responsible for getting you up in the morning—no amount of alarm clocks or wake-up calls are enough. Having assured wake-up plans also puts your mind to rest about oversleeping, which will help you relax and get to sleep. If you want you can lay out all your clothes and get everything else ready, so that the next morning you have to think and do as little as possible.

IN THE BLINK OF AN EYE . . .

It all goes by so goddamn fast. Individual pieces may go in slow motion, like the ceremony, but somehow the day itself flies by at ludicrous speed. (In *Spaceballs*, the 1987 Mel Brooks spoof of *Star Wars*, 'ludicrous speed' is one step beyond 'ridiculous speed' and a straight blur past light speed.) Someone will be saying their goodbyes to you when it seems like they just said hello. When you ask them why they're leaving so soon, you'll notice that others are getting their coats and the bar is closing. It's wedding relativity: the only thing that moves faster than light is good times.

The Moment and the Make-up

'The radiance of a truly happy bride is so beautifying that even a plain girl is made pretty, and a pretty one divine' (Post 1922, Chapter XXII). Great news for all those plain girls out there.

It's a rare, unfortunate man who isn't awestruck when he sees his bride walking down the aisle. It's impossible for us blokes to fully appreciate all the work that went into producing that moment. Hours and hours spent looking for a dress, finding the right shoes, manicures, pedicures, tanning beds, chemical peels, hair styling and, of course, make-up.

So, when you and your bride come face to face, don't be surprised if she's wearing a *tad* more make-up than usual (think kilos), along with fake eyelashes and other accoutrements. This is normal. It helps make her look stunning and, even more importantly, to *feel* stunning. It also works well for the photos and makes her look last through a very long day.

Still, some grooms find it disconcerting, especially if the bride doesn't usually wear much make-up, because she looks *different* to the girl he knows. It's also possible for wedding make-up to go too far (there's looking good in photos and there's looking like a Kings Cross tranny). No matter what you may think—and I cannot stress this enough—your bride is *absolutely beautiful* and that's what you tell her. Anything less would be crushing after all the effort she put into looking her very best.

In a Fog or in the Zone

During your wedding, you may experience a foggy feeling. Everything around you is happening at a slightly greater than normal speed, as if you're on strong cold medicine. You space out during conversations. You nod and smile a lot (like an idiot), but everyone is charmed by how stupidly happy you look. For other grooms, it's like being 'in the zone' when playing sport. You're not thinking about bending your knees, when to release, or how much arc to give the shot. You're just letting go—completely unconscious—and the shots are dropping like they don't have a choice. The next thing you know, the buzzer sounds and it's all over. You're still in another stratosphere and it takes a while to come down.

There Goes the Bride

Your bride may have her own mental paroxysm on the day. One New Age wedding book discusses a sense of 'walking through a dream' as part of a transition from maiden to wife: '[T]he initiate is at once *leaving being* and *coming into being* as she waits in a timeless, empty holding space' (Paul 2000, pp. 139–40). I haven't the foggiest idea what that means, but it could be a reference to the muscle relaxers she popped before the service (like Molly Ringwald's sister in *Sixteen Candles*) or the fact that she's eaten only rice cakes and air bubbles for the last two weeks to squeeze into that dress.

Time Ain't on Your Side

Because there's never enough time at a reception, things can easily get away from you. It's important to have a schedule and timing of events (sitting down for the meal, toasts, cutting the cake, dancing, etc.). The main players, like the venue managers and the MC, need to know that timetable and they should worry about managing it on the day, not you. There's no need to follow the schedule with military precision, but if you let the day wander by aimlessly you could give short shrift to something important like dancing to the 'Theme from *The Greatest American Hero* (Believe It or Not)'—come on, you know you love it.

GETTING THROUGH THE DAY

These are just a few tips and guidelines on getting through the day itself.

Needs No Introductions

I'm not a big fan of formal wedding party introductions at the reception. It's a bit too *Price is Right* ('Come on down!'). Of course, your bride or her family may insist (see '"Smart Bomb" Veto' box). And I say, if you're going to do it, then go all out and give the vital stats: 'Jessica is your maid of honour, she's 24, single and a Pisces. She likes long walks on the beach, stimulating conversation and tired clichés.' It gives your reception that meat-market quality which, let's face it, they have anyway.

> ### 'SMART BOMB' VETO
>
> Do you remember the old video games like Defender? You'd be shooting things like crazy but, when overwhelmed by foes, you had a few 'smart bombs' that would wipe out all your enemies on the screen. My brother managed to negotiate three 'smart bomb' vetos for his wedding—three things he could nullify without dispute. In the end he only deployed one, and that was used to wipe out the wedding party introductions.

This brings me to a broader point. Wedding books and mags make lots of cheesy suggestions, like placing written expressions of your love or one-word descriptions of what you value in each other on every table at your reception. While things that seem romantic to you (or your bride) may be touching to some guests, they will make others physically ill, like all your mates. There is a time and place for sentimentality (the ceremony and the toasts), but there's a thin line between love and vomit. Know that line and don't cross it.

Eat Me, Don't Drink Me (Too Much)

On the big day you should have some breakfast, even if you don't feel like it. If nerves have stolen your appetite, just keep it simple (good to do in any respect, as you don't want to risk any gastric upsets). It's like before the Big Game. You don't want to eat, but you need to keep your strength up. You don't want to get dizzy at the altar, and you *really* don't want to drink on an empty stomach.

It goes without saying that neither you nor your bride should be slobbering drunks at your reception (a rare occasion when I agree with the wedding books). It douses the mood just a smidgen. You may be so busy talking to people, mingling and doing the required reception activities that you have little time to grab any food, but drinks will magically slip into your fingers. If you're not eating much, those drinks will sneak up on you like a croc on a flailing tourist. Know yourself and your drinking limits. As a backup, assign one of your groomsmen to keep an eye on you and one of the bridesmaids to do the same for your bride, including *making you both eat*. If they drop the hint to put the glass down, take it.

The Dance

My partner and I are okay on our feet, so we didn't practise our first dance and just winged it (or wung it). Just don't embarrass yourself. If you're hopeless, then get lessons. If you don't know if you're hopeless, ask friends and relatives.

Your loved ones are always best at pointing out your short-comings. At one friend's wedding I could actually see the groom mouthing 'one, two, three, four' as he made his way around the dance floor, but he didn't trip over his feet, or the bride's, so the lessons paid off. Another tip: if you're nervous, ask your wedding party to join you on the dance floor after a minute, which will limit your time in the spotlight.

WEDDING NIGHT

This is another case where traditions and stereotypes of the past butt heads with the realities of the present. Today, people are not getting married as much in their late teens and early twenties. For this reason, along with loosening sexual mores, most people are not virgins on their wedding night. I have not studied the decline of maiden virginity to any great extent (beyond personal experience). My theory is that it started going out the window with World War I and the sequel. Young ladies of the day figured, not unreasonably, that the only thing worse than the loss of their premarital virginity was a young man dying a virgin in the jungles of the Pacific (or perhaps they were concerned that the local girls would do what they wouldn't). If Aussie girls didn't see this themselves, I'm sure the young soldiers didn't fail to point it out. War is hell . . . but it gets men laid. Probably why we keep having it.

(Not) Makin' Whoopee

This is the most fun I've ever had giving you wood (Homer Simpson).

Unfortunately, Homer was referring to a giant bag of popsicle sticks and not his wedding night with Marge. Several surveys confirm my anecdotal discussions with newlyweds that sex on the wedding night is getting rarer (perhaps as few as a fifth of couples). Moreover, most couples who consummated on their wedding night said it wasn't exactly the best sex of their lives—in fact, it was among the worst. Still, as the line goes, 'Sex is kinda like pizza. When it's bad, it's still pretty good' (from the 1994 film *Threesome*). So, what's interfering with the great romantic climax (pun intended) of your wedding?

It's no big mystery: the answer is sheer exhaustion. Typically, months of planning, organisation and stress have gone into the wedding, on top of all the normal stresses of work, life and family. The last week can be particularly hectic, with final preparations and subsidiary gatherings like rehearsal dinners, bucks' and hens' nights, etc. Let's add to that whatever crash diet regime your bride has been on, which probably leaves her vulnerable to a stiff breeze. That's all before the wedding day itself, with the emotion of the ceremony and the eating, drinking, dancing and merry-making of the reception. Increasingly, couples are tagging on an afterparty too, which may carry on into the wee hours.

When you finally get back to 'the honeymoon suite', it takes 45 minutes and a bit of struggle to get your bride out of her wedding dress with all its buttons, hooks, hoops, tapes, glue and staples. The whole thing leaves you and your bride physically, mentally and emotionally drained. After all that, it's hard to imagine any couple doing the deed without chemical stimulants (not that I'm making suggestions).

Don't force it. It's not going to be a great experience if it's done out of a sense of obligation. Instead, crash and have a go at morning sex. Alternatively, if you two are really keen on wedding night hijinks, then plan accordingly. Don't have a reception that ends late and don't go to any afterparties.

16

THE REST

*You're F@$#ing Kidding Me,
There's More?*

'Just when I thought I was out, they pull me back in'
(Michael Corleone (Al Pacino),
The Godfather: Part III).

. . . If you knew what went into an Italian wedding,
you'd understand.

Not everything on which I pontificate in this book fell neatly into one of the preceding chapters. This chapter is a catchall to cover any wedding-related program activities that haven't been addressed elsewhere, like the gift registry, invitations, the dreaded thankyou notes, and the highly anticipated honeymoon.

GIFTS

> Yet, among younger brides, a kind of underground 'rule' has recently emerged stating that guests should pay as much for their gifts as their meals will cost the hosts (Shervan and Sniechowski 2005, p. 186).

Of course that's silly, something even *The Smart Couple's Guide* recognises. It goes on to talk about 'the mature grace of conscious receiving' and I don't have a damn clue what that means. I do know that most guests purchase the wedding gift *before* the wedding, so how would they know what their meal is going to cost? Even if they purchase the gift after the wedding, are they going to sit at the reception adding up the cost of each course? Definitely not. The amount spent on the gift should depend, first, on the giver's means and, second, on the nature of their relationship to the couple. You can expect something nicer from your older, successful brother than from your second cousin on the dole. In any case, I hope you're not getting hitched for the gifts.

Cash Money

'Never, under any circumstances, mention that you'd prefer cash . . . I get cold chills just thinking about it' (Weatherly

2005, p. 97). Apparently, wedding planners get the chills whenever cash goes to anyone but them. Yet another case where we need to take a sledgehammer to outdated etiquette. The fact is, couples are getting married later in life. According to ABS statistics for Australia, the median age at first marriage rose from 23.3 to 31.6 for grooms and 20.9 to 29.3 for brides between 1974 and 2008. The idea of providing home-making gifts for the young newlyweds moving into their first home together is fading fast (though it's a fine thing to do in such cases). Couples marrying in their late twenties and early thirties don't need another bloody toaster. So, if that's you it's absolutely fine to suggest cash as a wedding gift, but here are a few tips on how to go about it.

1. *'Wish You Well'.* Some couples have a decorative 'wishing well' at their wedding: a miniature well with a slot where guests drop in an envelope with a card and their contribution (cash or cheque). Wishing wells can be purchased or rented from a number of sources (just Google 'wedding wishing wells'). At Italian weddings the bride often carries a little bag (*la borsa*) which serves the same purpose.

2. *I'd like (you) to make a deposit.* In these modern times, couples can provide bank account details to their guests to make a bank transfer, although that can make it harder to track contributions. Make sure to asks guests to note who the transfer is from. Also, it's considered crass to include gift details on the invitation itself, particularly bank details. You can

include a separate card in the envelope that provides details about the gift registry or provides bank details for a monetary gift.

3. *Have a porpoise.* It's a good idea to designate some purpose for your cash contributions. Whether it be some aspect of your honeymoon (like swimming with the dolphins), buying new furniture for your home or getting a nice piece of artwork, it makes the guests feel that they're contributing to something tangible. It also makes it easier to write the thank-you notes ('thanks for the hundred bucks' falls a little flat).

4. *Toaster from Aunt Tilly.* As some people are uncomfortable gifting cash, particularly among the older generations, you may want to have a small gift registry too, or at least provide some gift ideas to your parents so they can pass them on to older relatives and family friends who are uncomfortable giving money.

5. *Don't double dip.* While it's certainly okay to provide the *option* of a gift registry *or* giving cash (we did, as there were some things we wanted for the home), it should be clear that it's *one or the other.* Don't hit people up twice by asking for gifts *and* cash at the wedding. That's really poor form.

Gift Registry

You'd think that picking out essentially free stuff at a store would be fun, until you spend all day in a crowded department store, surrounded by tourists and shrill, screaming children, deciding which napkin rings *truly reflect you as a*

DISCRETION IS THE BETTER PART OF STUPIDITY

'You should never make any sort of announcement concerning your registries. This includes save-the-dates, invitations and websites . . . The only appropriate way to spread the word about your registries is through the grapevine' (Weatherly 2005, p. 97). That's galactically stupid. Everyone knows your guests are getting you a wedding gift. Your guests want the information about your preferred gifting options. Why would you make it as difficult as possible for them to get that information? How is that polite or considerate? Let's drop the bullshit pretence here and just give the guests the gift info.

couple. If your bride insists on dragging you along, break up the gift picking into multiple sessions. The typical groom comes undone about one to two hours in, and it's going to take longer than that. If you can swing it, have your bride do a once through without you, so she's narrowed things down before she brings you in for your thoughts (such as they are). Lastly, it makes things much easier for the guests, and you, if your registry is online, whether that's through a department store or a purely online gift registry (e.g. www.weddinggiftsdirect.com.au, www.weddinglistco.com.au, and www.yourgiftwish.com.au).

Groom Registry

Modern wedding books urge men to get more involved in their wedding until you get to the *bridal* registry chapter, and that's exactly what it is. If it's really *our* wedding, why can't there be a few things for the blokes? Most of it goes to china sets, silverware and crystal vases. You'll get thrown a bone or two, with beer or scotch glasses, but that's just a sneak attempt at civilising us. I mean, drinking out of the bottle never bothered us before (though the scotch does tend to dribble down one's shirt). I think it's fair and reasonable to ask for a few items (or one big one) on the whole list that are really for you: electronics, a barbecue, sports equipment, etc. Admittedly, 'fair and reasonable' rarely come into wedding planning but you could get lucky, in which case I offer a few ideas for the *groom* registry:

1. *Wide-screen TV.* Brotherly love is all well and good, but a big new TV is the best gift one man can give another.
2. *Stereo surround sound.* I am man, hear my electronics roar.
3. *Blue-ray DVD player.* You won't be able to tell the difference, but it doesn't matter.
4. *Sony PlayStation 3.* Blue-ray DVD is included, and it sounds more manly than 'Wii'.
5. *Pool table.* You better have a shed, because she ain't letting it in the living room.
6. *Season tickets.* I'm not talking ballet.
7. *Nice poker set.* Now that you're married, the toothpicks just won't do.
8. *Golf clubs.* Whether you play or not, it gives you an excuse to get out of the house for a few hours.
9. *Power tools.* Why *be* a tool when you can *own* a tool?

You may not find all such items on traditional wedding registries, in which case you can register for them separately or send your list to a few close male relatives and friends.

SNAIL MAIL'S LAST PURPOSE

A wedding is probably the only time that anyone bothers to lick an envelope and slap on the stamp any more.

Invitations

Getting wedding invitations with calligraphy means ordering them at least four months before your wedding and it will cost north of $2000, easy. If you make that one aspect of your wedding so difficult, the whole process is going to be very painful. Invitations are one place you can simplify and save. It's not hard to do your own with a trip to the stationery store and a reasonable quality printer. Alternatively, a graphic designer friend or rellie with Photoshop skills may be willing to help. Remember, this is something guests will keep on their fridge for a while then throw away. There may be people that put all the wedding invitations they ever get into a big scrapbook, but you probably don't want to hang out with them.

Addresses

Track down addresses as soon as you finalise your guest list. Most people respond right away, but it takes a while for all the addresses to trickle in. Etiquette mavens would shudder at the thought of an informal 'save-the-date' for your wedding, but it's silly to think that when asking

'SAVE-THE-DATE'

A 'save-the-date' notice is basically a pre-invitation to your wedding. It lets people know, even before the formal invite arrives, that you're getting married, that they're invited (or are about to be) and the planned date, so the would-be guests can mark it off in their calendar and ensure to make no other plans. It can be a good thing to do, as the invitations don't usually go out until a few months before the wedding and people can make their plans far ahead these days, especially around school holidays or long weekends. Traditionally, the save-the-date would be another formal mailing with a brief notecard (a friend of mine used a library book notecard with a due date on it for the wedding date, which I thought was pretty clever). However, it can be hard enough to do the invitations without adding to your mailing burden, and I think things have relaxed enough that a 'save-the-date' by email won't offend anyone who's modern enough to be using email.

for addresses you wouldn't say what they're for ('hey, I need your address, but I can't tell you why, unless I use parchment and quill'). So, if you know the date of the wedding, you might as well mention it in your email or phone conversation and the address collection process can act as an informal heads-up on the wedding date.

RSVP (Respond or Suffer Vicious Pounding)

Inevitably, there will be people who don't RSVP to your wedding by the prescribed date. It can be frustrating, but at this point it's safe to either call or email these folks to chase up their response. Calling is the most effective way to get an immediate answer and it shouldn't take long to chase the stragglers down. You may even learn that the invitation never reached a few of the guests for whatever reason.

I Just Want to Thank You

Unless you're the luckiest groom in the world or have taken on some other onerous task, chances are you're going to have to write some portion of the thankyou notes—especially for your own friends and family. Here's what you may *want* to write but can't:

Dear Cheap-Arse,

I will be sure to think of you as I scrub my under-carriage with your generous gift of a hand towel. You clearly didn't realise that you were supposed to get the whole *set* of towels, not just the smallest piece. Hey, it's no big deal, because that salmon you scarfed down just cost $100 a plate and you only drank your body weight in booze. We'll be sure to bring along a nice alcopop to the next dinner at your place, then eat your nice food and drink all your wine.

Yours gratefully,
Mr and Mrs Gorgeous Couple

For your *real* thankyou notes I have provided a step-by-step example with instructions, including optional touches. The example covers a multitude of circumstances, so no individual note will need to be this long.

Dear John and Kate {thank you for having such bland, easy-to-spell names},

Thank you for coming to Sydney for our wedding {first, thank them for coming, noting if they travelled}. It meant a great deal to have you there {nice platitude}. We are especially grateful to you for being a groomsman in our wedding and for all of your help with the day {note any special service to your wedding (if not thanked in a separate note), such as being a wedding attendant, hosting out-of-town guests, helping you make the invitations, etc.}. Your support and friendship mean a lot to us {optional: add something meaningful for close friends and family}.

Thank you also for your generous gift of the wine glasses and carafe {identify the gift and thank them for it, calling it 'generous', 'kind', 'thoughtful', etc., even if it's not generous or actually sucks}. We recently joined the Wine Society to learn more about wine, so we'll get good use out of your gift {optional: say something about how you will use the gift}.

Love {yes, you sign off 'love' even with your mates, but it's from both of you, so it's okay},
He-Man & She-Ra {I personally like the '&' for hand-written sign-offs even though I have trouble writing it, but you can go with 'and' if you like (my editors have for this book)}

Yes, you have to *hand write* the thankyou notes (and definitely not use email). I'm no slave to etiquette, but there's something lame and thoughtless about a typed or emailed thankyou note, and this is coming from a man with the handwriting of an eight-year-old on Red Bull. Just do the notes while distracted by some passive activity like watching cricket, which leaves plenty of gaps for scribbling. They'll probably be done by the third day of the Test. If you want to go the extra mile, include a wedding photo of yourselves with the note and, for special folks, a good photo of them from the wedding. If you have the negatives or high-quality digital copies of your photos (see Chapter 7), it's easy and cheap to get prints at your local photo shop.

No-gifters

What do you do about the no-gifters: people who show at your wedding, eat your food, drink your booze and don't have the decency to get you a monogrammed waffle iron? My wife reckons you write them a thankyou note anyway, and thank them for coming to the wedding. This didn't make much sense to me; but women are more sly than men, because getting the thankyou note reminds or guilts the slackers into getting the gift. In that case, I refuse to send out *another* thankyou note once the gift arrives (I recognise that's technically bad form, but it's one 'thankyou' per customer for me).

DOWN WITH THE ONE-YEAR RULE

Etiquette mavens differ on the one-year window for wedding gifts, but it's a ridiculous concept in the modern age. You certainly don't show up to a mate's forty-first birthday party with that special bottle of scotch for his fortieth. Annoyingly, the year's allowance keeps you from putting away the thankyou cards as you wait for the stragglers' gifts to trickle in. Moreover, if the guests wait too long the gift registry will be closed down, and they'll likely get you something that you neither need nor want. Meanwhile, you've had to purchase items off your own registry, particularly to complete a set. The best thing for a guest to do is get the damn gift as soon as the invite arrives. It's pretty easy these days with online registries—they just pick something off the list in their price range. It doesn't matter what, because they know you want everything on there. If you're a guy, like me, and you don't buy the gift right away, you *will* forget. I've avoided speaking to certain friends because I was ashamed that I never got them a wedding gift and it seemed way too late and too awkward to get them one by that point.

Wedding Favours

What are we, ten? Wedding favours are another item that falls in the category of not doing anything done at a child's birthday party. If you (or your bride) really want to do it, because some gift idea fits with 'the theme' of your wedding, go nuts; but in a budget rife with tough decisions, favours shouldn't be a priority. A lot of little things add up. One less costly idea is to give guests a CD of some music from your wedding (a 'mix tape'). It violates any number of copyright laws, but it's inexpensive and it's a personal reminder of your wedding. Just don't put 'The Chicken Dance', 'Macarena' or Justin Bieber on it if you want to maintain your dignity among your mates.

SHOWERS

'Why not try a couple's shower so the guys won't miss out on all the fun?' (Weatherly 2005, p. 100). Really, no thanks, please. Not on our account. No, no, thank you. Please, for the love of God, *no*!

Unfortunately, couple's showers are gaining in popularity (there are even grooms' showers, though they need a more manly name, like beer parties). However, *bridal* showers are still the norm, so you probably won't have to go. Also, showers are hosted by friends or family of the bride (or couple), so there shouldn't be too much for you to do other than show up and get stuff, with *one major caveat*: shower gifts also require thankyou notes (it never ends).

Showers are supposed to be small gatherings with close family and friends, bearing in mind that anyone invited to a shower should be invited to the wedding. Like your wedding, the shower may have a 'theme', which often ties into suggested gifts. It might be a *MasterChef* shower, where guests bring exotic ingredients, favourite recipes, a bottle of wine, etc. You might prefer a barbecue or golf theme, but as the groom you'll have to go with the flow. Unfortunately, you and the boys won't be invited to a shower with a lingerie theme, but hey, that's what concealed webcams are for.

REHEARSAL DINNER

Rehearsal dinners are more common in the US than Australia, but it's always an option. They're traditionally hosted by your parents but this isn't set in stone, especially if your parents are contributing in other ways. It's usually held the night before the wedding, after the wedding rehearsal, but that's not ironclad either. (If it is the night before, make sure it doesn't end too late—and NO afterparties!) The main rule is that it shouldn't be more formal, lavish or in any way outdo the wedding reception. As always, let your circumstances be your guide. We had a casual barbecue at my sister-in-law's place several days before the wedding, because that made the most sense for us.

The main point of the rehearsal dinner (or breakfast, lunch or brunch) is for the families to get to know each other better and spend time with the wedding party in a more intimate setting. Inviting nearly the whole guest list defeats this purpose. Some couples or parents feel an obligation to invite out-of-town guests, but that's unnecessary (unless they're partners of people in the wedding party, whom you may want to invite anyway). I'm sure your out-of-town guests can find something to occupy themselves for the evening (for the hopeless, you can recommend restaurants and activities for them on your website or in an email). You could also have a smaller dinner and invite the blow-ins for drinks afterwards.

The rehearsal dinner is a great time for toasting and roasting, and that's always fun (even though it's you on the flame). It's a good opportunity for people who won't get to toast at the wedding. It also allows for longer toasts, with stories, anecdotes or a slideshow that would be too long for the reception.

THE NAME GAME

What if your bride doesn't want to take your surname? Would she be 'Julia Gulia' (the potential married name of Drew Barrymore's character in *The Wedding Singer* if she'd gone through with marrying Glen, the philandering junk-bond trader) or 'Philippa Butts'? I figured my partner's name is her call. On the other hand, I do take issue with hyphenating the kids' names. It's fine in theory, but in practice Wojakowski-Stephanopoulos doesn't exactly fit on the back of a sports jersey. Moreover, what happens when your kid get married to a Von Hoffstedder-Di Francesco? Do their kids become 'Wojakowski-Stephanopoulos-Von Hoffstedder-Di Francesco'? The politically correct folks don't seem to look past the first generation. Another questionable plan is to give the boys your name and the girls her name. First, you don't know the gender of your future children; it could be all girls or all boys. Second, then the outside world doesn't recognise your kids as brother and sister, which is weird for all concerned.

HONEYMOON

'In the Middle Ages, mead . . . was drunk by the bride and groom for thirty days . . . During this period, the couple stayed hidden from their parents and friends, the mead no doubt loosening their inhibitions and getting the marriage off to an auspicious start' (Post 2006, p. 378). You heard the nice etiquette lady: go medieval, get drunk and screw.

Honeymoon planning traditionally falls within the groom's domain. These days brides are likely to be more involved but you'll probably still take the lead, and fair enough, as she's likely doing the lion's share of wedding planning. Just make sure it's something you will *both* enjoy. If your bride has nightmares about horrible insects laying eggs under her skin, an African safari isn't a good idea (bearing in mind that you'll catch the grief for her suffering). If you have completely different ideas, try to go to a destination where it's possible to both get some time doing what you want. Importantly, *keep a keen eye on the wedding budget if you want anything left for the honeymoon.* Budget plans also mean you need a general idea of what you're doing for your honeymoon, and a general idea of costs, relatively early in your wedding planning.

Leave of Absence

The tyranny of distance has made Australians great world travellers. If there was ever a moment to take some time and see the world, your honeymoon is it. You have your careers stretched out ahead of you and children waiting in the wings, ready to take over your lives. This could be your last chance to take that trip you always wanted. So it's worth it to see if you can both get extended leave from your employers. The worst they can do is say no. Both my bride and I were between jobs at the time and had some money saved, so we travelled around Europe for over two months before visiting the US to see my family.

Communication

Remember, the aim of any great trip is to make your friends and loved ones jealous—to the point that they wish they were you. Otherwise, it's just not worth doing. So, take lots of pictures, set up a blog for your trip, send regular emails, update your Facebook page, tweet or what have you. Let them know what a good time you're having and they're not.

Planning

This is not a travel guide, and as the possibilities for your honeymoon are endless I couldn't possibly provide detailed information on honeymoon planning. There are many good travel books and websites out there and I suggest that you rely on those for planning your honeymoon rather than any wedding book (you don't ask the plumber to fix your wiring). TripAdvisor (www.tripadvisor.com) is a good resource to check up on hotels before you book, and can also help you find cheap rates. The ratings are based on guest reviews, and while you can't trust every review it tends to be right in the aggregate. In particular, it's worth investing in a travel book once you've chosen your destination or region (Lonely Planet, if you want to buy Australian). That said, I do have some general tips for planning and enjoying your honeymoon.

Helter Skelter

You and your bride may be up for an adventure holiday (hiking, biking, spelunking, etc.) or a whirlwind European tour, but try to build in some chill time, especially if you're heading off right after your wedding. The build-up to a wedding is massive; after that you need some time to be *still*. A few days on the beach or in a lakeside cabin before you climb Kilimanjaro is all I'm asking. Similarly,

> **BIKE TOUR-TURE**
>
> While a bike tour sounds romantic, I wouldn't recommend making it the principal part of your honeymoon. Let's just say it's not very conducive to consummating the marriage, as the saddle-soreness sidelines both of you from bed gymnastics for the duration.

if you're having your honey-moon a few weeks or months after the wedding (as we did), give yourselves a mini-break immediately after the wedding. My wife regretted going back to work right away because she was exhausted after the wedding weekend.

It's also good to have a combination of planning and spontaneity in your honey-moon. It gets tiresome finding a hotel every time you arrive in a new city. On the other hand, if everything is rigidly planned you can feel trapped by your schedule and miss out on those unexpected opportunities that can be the most memorable part of your trip.

Don't Overpack

The temptation for a long trip is to want something (or, in your bride's case, four things) for every possible occasion or circumstance. Bear two things in mind. First, airlines are getting very strict about weight limits on checked and carry-on luggage, particularly discount airlines. It can be as little as 20 kilos *total* for checked luggage and 7 kilos for carry-on, and the penalties are per *kilo* and univer-sally insane. For example, a Qantas economy passenger is limited to 23 kilos on flights to and from Europe, with a penalty of *$50 per kilo* for excess luggage. That means 29 kilos of luggage could cost you an extra $300. Second, if you're travelling around a bit you really don't want to be dragging more than 20 kilos with you. Not every train station has escalators and it's not always possible (or afford-able) to catch taxis everywhere. Of course, the hard part is convincing your new wife to limit her travelling wardrobe (it's the damn shoes). Good luck!

Travel Agent

The decision to use a travel agent is like the decision to use a wedding planner: it depends on the complexity and length of your honeymoon and how much time you have to devote to planning. If you want to spend two weeks at a self-contained, luxury beach resort, then you can probably sort that yourself. If you're taking a few weeks or months off to travel through multiple countries and you have little spare time for travel planning, then a travel agent can be very helpful. Short of going to an independent travel agency, your credit-card company may have travel-planning services. Travel agents are also good for telling you about visa require-ments, vaccinations, travel insurance and other things you may need for your trip.

'To Everything There is a Season'

It's important to look into the weather and other seasonal factors for potential travel destinations. Remember, it's overcast and rainy in London from January through to December, so you may want to avoid it then. Also, if you see a fantastic deal on an incredible holiday destination it's a warning that you could be flying into prime cyclone season or a military coup, so check before you book.

Travel Insurance

If you're travelling overseas, travel insurance is a *necessity*. If something goes wrong in an unfamiliar place you want to know that you're both covered. However, for an extended honeymoon to multiple destinations, travel insurance can be expensive. Before you pay for it, check to see if one of your credit-card companies provides it for free if you book flights on your card. Credit-card booking fees are annoying, but the fee is probably much less than what you would end up paying for travel insurance.

It's Not All Sunshine and Roses

Like your wedding, if you're doing a long trip that involves extensive travel you can guarantee that some things will go wrong: you'll miss a train, a hotel won't have your reservation, you'll get some foul weather, etc. These things happen, but if you accept that going in and don't let it get to you then it won't ruin your holiday. As with the wedding, it's your *attitude* towards these little misadventures, not the events themselves, that makes or breaks your honeymoon. So, make the best of it, try to enjoy yourselves, and the next day will (hopefully) go better—or at least you'll have a good story.

Apartments

If you're staying in a city for a week or, in some cases, more than a few days, renting a short-term apartment can be a good, economical option. Not only is it often cheaper than a hotel, but you get some basic kitchen facilities, which allows you to cook to save money or when you're tired of eating out. Sometimes you also get a washer and dryer, which makes it easier to wash your clothes during extended trips.

Flashpacking

If you're planning a longer honeymoon and don't have the scratch for extended five-star luxury but don't want to travel like backpackers, why not be *flashpackers*? It's a relatively new and contested term describing people who travel a step or two up from backpackers. Stay at cheap and moderately priced hotels (i.e., you have your own room and bathroom) or rent inexpensive apartments, as opposed to crashing at backpacker hovels. Fly to travel longer distances, but use discount airlines or go economy. You get the idea. It's not the royal treatment, but you have comfortable, cosy, clean travel and you can always splurge on one particular part of your trip (e.g., a top restaurant, a few days at a luxury resort).

You Wouldn't Like Me When I'm Grumpy

On an extended trip together, you're both likely to get grumpy with each other at various times because you're tired, hungry, drunk, dirty, wet, etc. Welcome to married life! Try to spot the warning signs in yourself and your new wife and head off the root cause (get some food, rest, shelter, etc.). Otherwise, ride it out and try to forgive each other quickly. You're stuck with each other now so you'll both have to get over it, and you don't want a fight spoiling a whole day of your honeymoon (or multiple days).

General Tips

These are just some general planning tips, particularly for overseas travel, but you should consult a reputable travel guide, website or agent for more detailed advice:

1. *Passports.* Make sure your passports are in order. Note that some countries may refuse you entry if your passport expires within six months of your arrival, so if that's an issue have it renewed before you leave. Also, check on the visa requirements for every country you're travelling to or through (or *could* travel to). It can take some time for visas to be processed, so don't leave this to the last minute.

2. *Shots (needles and bullets).* Consult your doctor for any additional vaccinations you may need before travelling abroad or medication you should take with you. If you're taking medication with you, be sure to bring copies of your prescription and, if there's any doubt, confirm that it's not illegal to possess or bring the medication into any of the countries you'll be visiting or passing through. If you're travelling to less stable regions or countries, check the Department of Foreign Affairs and Trade website (www.dfat.gov.au) for travel warnings and advisories (registering with DFAT is also a good idea).

3. *Cash stash.* For emergencies, take some travellers cheques that you keep separate from the rest of your money. It's a good idea to keep one credit card separate too. Also, make sure you have plenty of cash available in an accessible bank account.

4. *Documents.* Make copies of important documents (passport, driver's licence, etc.) and leave them with someone in Australia, or make a PDF copy and email them to yourself so you'll have access to them if you lose the originals during your trip. Also check to see if you'll need an international driver's licence where you're travelling (you can get one from the motoring club in your state).

5. *Tickets please.* Have an itinerary with dates and the contact details of hotels, tour operators, etc. Take it with you and give copies to family members, friends or colleagues who may need to get in touch with you. Have printouts of your e-tickets, hotel reservation confirmations, etc.

Finally, enjoy yourselves. You got through it and you deserve it.

EPILOGUE

It's been three years now since my nuptials. That's how long it's taken to write this book and settle the various legal disputes amidst all my other pursuits (lingerie salesman and border collie trainer).

I've been spending money wildly in anticipation of the global phenomenon that *The Last Decision You'll Ever Make* (or 'TLD', as I'm calling it) is sure to become. Beyond the prodigious book sales, of course, is the rampant and exploitative merchandising: *The Last Decision* t-shirts, coffee mugs, pens, parachutes, prenup agreements, and so on. Hopefully you've bought many copies by now, and perhaps a t-shirt or two, or I'm going to have to write another book to pay for this yacht.

As for my marriage, I can't say enough about it. For one, it's still there, despite the fact that I wrote this book. That says a great deal about the patience, forbearance and understanding of my wife—except for the fact that I've hidden numerous pages from her. As I mentioned earlier, being married is a good thing—it's like right before you were married, but you don't have to deal with a wedding any more.

Of course, other challenges come. It's not easy to afford a house in this world (at least, not the one you want), especially when one of you leaves his high-paying corporate law job to write a niche-market book for three years. There are job stresses, family stresses, trying-to-get-pregnant stresses, being-pregnant stresses, children stresses, child-care stresses, and so on.

You learn quickly that every stress in your life also becomes a stress on your marriage. In fact, your marriage too easily becomes a repository for all your stress, because of a quirk in human nature that means we tend to place our frustrations on the person who least deserves it—the one who is there for us above all others.

It is the easiest thing in the world to take your wife for granted, and for her to do the same—so don't. Talk to each other and listen to each other, always. If you don't know how (and many people don't), then learn. A lifetime is a long time, and it's hard to make it work. It takes persistence, perseverance, resilience and forgiveness. It takes both of you.

Good luck, be well and stay tuned for my next book, on the joys of pregnancy: *The Breathing is Bullshit.*

REFERENCES

I have quoted from a number of traditional wedding books throughout this book. In general, I do this to mock their advice or to distinguish my own point of view from those entrenched in the wedding industry. The full reference to each book is noted below.

I should add that while I poke fun at the traditional wedding literature, not everything they have to say is all bad and I would certainly not recommend using this book as your only guidance to planning your wedding *as a couple*. This is more of a supplement so that a groom, who will never read the traditional wedding books, can have some idea of what's going on, and to inject a little levity and perspective into the process for both of you.

If I were to recommend any traditional wedding book, it would have to be *Emily Post's Wedding Etiquette*. Despite the very traditional origins of the book (the author, Peggy Post, is the great-grand-daughter-in-law of Emily Post—the original maven of etiquette—continuing in her tradition and trade-mark) and the deceptive titles of some competing books that claim to be more modern, I found that Peggy Post's book gave the most practical and comprehensive guidance, had the most common-sense approach to etiquette and the least amount of bullshit. High praise indeed.

Bryant, Steve. *The Best Man's Pocket Guide*. London: Greenwich Editions, 2005.

Fowler, Shandon. *The Groom's Instruction Manual*. Philadelphia: Quirk Books, 2008.

Love, James [I kid you not]. *The Groom's Guide*. London: New Holland, 2007.

Paul, Sheryl. *The Conscious Bride: Women unveil their true feelings about getting hitched*. Oakland: New Harbinger, 2000.

Post, Emily. *Etiquette in Society, in Business, in Politics and at Home*. New York: Funk & Wagnalls, 1922. Available online at Bartleby.com: www.bartleby.com/95/.

Post, Peggy. *Emily Post's Wedding Etiquette* (5th edn). New York: HarperCollins, 2006.

Shaw, Kim. *The New Book of Wedding Etiquette: How to combine the best traditions with today's flair*. New York: Three Rivers Press, 2001.

Shervan, Judith and Sniechowski, James. *The Smart Couple's Guide to the Wedding of Your Dreams*. Novato, California: New World Library, 2005.

Weatherly, Laura. *Stop! Don't Plan a Wedding Without this Book*. New York: Alpha, 2005.

GENERAL REFERENCES

Chandra, Vikram. *Sacred Games*. London: Faber and Faber, 2007.

de Tocqueville, Alexis. *Democracy in America*. J.P. Mayer (ed.), George Lawrence (trans.). New York: HarperPerennial, 1988.

ACKNOWLEDGEMENTS

First and foremost, I would like to acknowledge and thank my wife, Charmayne ('Char', for those of us fortunate enough to know her best). As a proposal warm-up, I quit my high-paying law job to pursue an unspecified and non-lucrative career as a writer and political activist. Your patience, support and belief in me during the three years since sustained me through long days of work and long nights of self-doubt. You are my reason for everything.

I would like to thank my family and friends who either willingly or unwittingly supplied some of the stories for this book or who read and commented on the early chapters (particularly Char and my mother, Mary). A special thank-you goes to the Honourable Doctor Meredith Burgmann BA MA PhD, co-founder of the Ernie Awards for Sexist Remarks, for sweeping her misogynism detector over an early draft.

My friend and publisher, Jane Palfreyman, encouraged me when these 300 pages were a mere idea and shepherded me through from beginning to end. You are the best for a reason.

Thanks to the patience and kind attentions of my editor, Jo Lyons, my mere collection of words became a book. That book, from cover to cover, would not look or feel the same without the excellent design work of Lisa White. I also want to thank the rest of the team at Allen & Unwin for making this book what it is, which is much more than the words I have written.

Fiona Katauskas is a friend and a great Australian talent. This book would be so much less without her brilliant illustrations and her sparkling sense of humour. I'm so glad she could be a part of this with me.

Many thanks to my agent, Elizabeth Troyer, who took on an untried and untested author and showed him the way.

Finally, I would like to thank the Australasian Society of Primates (you know who you are) for making a young American lawyer believe he could write, be funny and cause trouble. It's all your fault. With thumbs we oppose!

APPENDIX

SAMPLE WEDDING BUDGET

ITEM	ESTIMATED COST	ACTUAL COST	OVER/ UNDER
Ceremony			
Beach	300	300	—
Carpet	230	230	—
Minister	350	350	—
Reception			
Food/drinks	5,000	5,500	500
Decorations/flowers	1,300	1,600	300
Transport	600	600	—
Wedding party			
Bride			
Dress and veil	1,000	1,250	250
Shoes	200	200	—
Jewellery	150	150	—
Bridesmaids			
Shoes	600	600	—
Groom and groomsmen	450	600	150
Photographer	700	1,200	500
Invitations/thankyou cards			
Invites/labels/postage	100	100	—
Thankyou cards	150	150	—
Music	1,000	1,350	350
Accommodation			
Wedding night	250	300	50
Wedding rings	1,500	1,250	–250
Other			
Bail for bucks' night	500	500	—
Reserve	1,500	1,500	—
Total	**15,880**	**17,730**	**1,850**